# Better Than Success
## 8 Principles of Faithful Leadership

C. Jeff Woods

Judson Press
Valley Forge

*Better Than Success: 8 Principles of Faithful Leadership*
© 2001 by Judson Press, Valley Forge, PA 19482–0851
All rights reserved.

Bible quotations in this volume are the New Revised Standard Version of the Bible, copyright © 1989 by the Division of Christian Education of the National Council of the Churches of Christ in the United States of America. Used by permission. All rights reserved.

Judson Press has made every effort to trace the ownership of all quotes. We regret any error made and will be pleased to make the necessary correction in future printings and editions of this book.

Library of Congress Cataloging-in-Publication Data

Woods, Charles Jeffrey, 1958-
    Better than success : 8 principles of faithful leadership / C. Jeff Woods.
        p.   cm.
    Includes bibliographical references (p. ).
    ISBN 0–8170–1389-X (pbk. : alk. paper)
    1. Christian leadership.  I. Title.

BV652.1 .W64 2001
253—dc21                                                                00–060370

Printed in the U.S.A.

07 06 05 04 03 02 01

10 9 8 7 6 5 4 3 2 1

# CONTENTS

# ACKNOWLEDGMENTS

MY WIFE, KANDY, AND MY CHILDREN, BRANDON AND Kelsey, are a joy to my life and an inspiration to my writing. My American Baptist colleagues provided both challenge and support as I wrestled with leadership issues among them. Chuck Armstrong was a great sounding board, adding substance to the echoes as we traveled the miles and talked about leadership. I owe much gratitude to Jeff Jones who reviewed the initial manuscript and offered many insights that became a part of the pages that lie ahead.

While several experiences helped hone my ideas, time spent with colleagues in the National Religious Leadership Program, funded by the Lilly Foundation, renewal time at the American Baptist Assembly, and discussions at the Jimmy Carter Center added significantly to my thinking and understanding of leadership in today's world.

# INTRODUCTION

**S**UCCESSFUL LEADERS MOBILIZE PEOPLE TO MAKE A difference in the world around them; faithful leaders mobilize people to make a difference in God's world. Successful leaders serve a bottom line; faithful leaders serve God. This is not just another book about striving for success as a leader. It is written specifically for Christian leaders who want to be faithful in all aspects of their Christian journey, including leadership.

As you will discover, faithfulness is not always consistent with success. Sometimes the most faithful task will not be the most successful task. Seeking after the world's praise does not always lead to praise from God. Serving God can actually make it difficult to please the world. Serving God can lead to a completely different set of rewards than one might normally expect to receive from being a successful leader. This reality can cause many to choose success over faithfulness. I believe that Christians, however, are called to be faithful in their leadership as well as their lives. Faithful leadership often involves going beyond what the successful leader might do in order to serve God. Faithful leaders strive to serve the one who initiated faithfulness, namely, God.

The ultimate model for faithful ministry is drawn from Jesus Christ. Jesus constantly sought to please God. Such intentions did not always lead to successful performance standards. Jesus regularly irritated the ruling class. He spent most of his time with the neediest rather than the most influential. People Jesus healed were told to keep silent about the miracles. He only recruited twelve followers. An earthly empire was his for the taking, but he chose the more faithful route to a cross. Jesus' only concern was remaining true to his calling. The successful route and faithful path are two distinct avenues. Sometimes the faithful path leads to persecution, neglect, even death.

This book has a different "bottom line" than most other books on leadership. The world consistently sets the standards for success. For the faithful leader, however, nothing else besides serving God really matters. Faithful leaders do not strive for faithfulness *and* success. They strive for faithfulness alone. It will not work to pursue both, believing that one is always capable of choosing the higher ground whenever success and faithfulness collide. Jesus warned about the impossibility of seeking after both God and mammon. Consistently striving to orient one's pathway toward God is the role of faithful leaders. Managers do things right. Leaders do the right thing. Effective leaders do the successful thing. Faithful leaders do God's thing.

## Successful Leadership

While participating in a seminar on the West Coast, I attended the worship service of a very large congregation. I enjoy visiting congregations that stretch my thinking about what it means to be a church in today's world. On this particular visit, I was told in advance that I would be visiting a "successful congregation." I was not disappointed. Every nuance of the congregation exuded success. I was greeted in the parking lot by parking-lot greeters. Additional greeters were positioned at every entrance. In the first few moments of my arrival, I was cordially welcomed several times in several settings. Visible signs proudly displayed the solitary mission statement of this congregation ... to promote success. Banners, pamphlets, bulletin boards, and handouts all left little doubt that this church wanted you to be successful. One particular banner declared, "God wants you to be successful in every way ... physically, emotionally, spiritually, financially." Another piece of print material explained, "If you are a Christian, God wants you to be successful. You deserve to be successful. What are you waiting for?"

Upon entering the sanctuary, I joined 5,000 others who had gathered for worship that Sunday morning. Upon mingling with a few people in the foyer, I quickly understood that those who had gathered were eager to learn about how to become a success in life. From the opening announcements to the closing song, we all were challenged to be successful. During the opening announcements, the pastor told the congregation that they had become so successful that it would be necessary for them to find a new location.

"You know that we have been growing by leaps and bounds," the pastor explained. "God has been blessing our efforts. Because of God's blessings, a few of us have been meeting to discuss a possible new location. In a few weeks the new location will be announced to you."

My thoughts roamed when the pastor reported that the new location would be announced to the membership. I knew I wasn't in Kansas anymore. Neither was I in one of my familiar American Baptist churches. This certainly was different. I reminded myself that I was in a successful church.

"A few of you may have a problem with the new location when it is announced," the pastor continued. "But, if you are praying in the right spirit, you will not have a problem with the announcement. During the next few weeks, I encourage you to pray carefully. Those who pray in the right spirit will not have a problem with the announcement."

My thoughts continued to roam, but you don't want to hear them at this point.

"Oh, I guess I'll go ahead and reveal the new location to you right now," the pastor teased. "All of you know that this city just loves us. So, they have decided to give us the old sports stadium after the new one is built!" Laughter ensued. "No, the team is doing so poorly right now that they have decided to give us the new stadium, and they will keep the old one until the team can start winning a few more games." Laughter overtook the room.

Following the announcements, we sang several praise songs, led by a very energetic band. The pastor stood up and began to talk again. I thought that he had begun the sermon. Then, I noticed that the choir was still standing behind him on the risers. Were they going to stand there through the entire sermon? Upon listening more carefully to the comments, it finally occurred to me that this was not the sermon. This was the introduction to the offering … a twenty-minute introduction to the offering! Many church treasurers right now are probably thinking, "This *must* be a successful church!"

Following the offering, a few more songs, and a few more announcements on video, the sermon commenced. The subject was (care to take a guess?), "You must have the right attitude in life in order to be successful." At the conclusion of the sermon a unique invitation was given to come forward. Although the content of the invitation was somewhat unique, "Anyone who does not currently have an attitude in his or her life that is leading to success will be encouraged to come forward," the bold delivery of the invitation completely overshadowed its content. The delivery consisted of a three-fold invitation. During the first phase, the pastor asked everyone to stand and join hands. Then he announced. "On the count of three, if you do not currently have an attitude in your life that is leading to success, squeeze the hand of the person next to you." On the count of three he screeched out, "Squeeze!" at full decibel. He yelled so loud that I am sure that several people squeezed the hand of the person next to them as an involuntary reaction to the noise. If you chose to squeeze, however, you were now locked in. During phase two, he announced, "On the count of three, if the person next to you squeezed your hand, raise up that person's hand!" Did you catch the switch to the neighbor? If you had squeezed the person's hand next to you, your neighbor was now being instructed to raise up your hand. Would that have upset you? It's not over yet. In one brief moment you will be walking down the aisle. "On the count of three," the pastor continued as he explained phase three, "if your hand is raised, come forward!" To no surprise, people flooded the aisle ways. As the mass of people stood down front, the pastor looked right into the television monitors and said, "See these decisions today? You need to give to this ministry because of these *salvation* decisions!"

As I returned to my seminar that afternoon, each participant was invited to relate his or her Sunday-morning worship experiences. I think I had the floor for three hours! I had been to similar worship services before as a means of stretching my thinking. This one was by far the most contrary to my own principles of leadership. It was that particular worship service that convinced me of the need to write a book on faithful leadership.

Successful leaders learn various leadership skills that allow them to direct a group of people toward a specific cause. Sometimes that cause is honorable. Sometimes it is dishonorable. Sometimes the cause is for the public good. Sometimes the cause is for private gain. Regardless of the content of the goal, reaching it is what makes a leader successful. Analyzing the nature of the goal as well as the means of getting there, however, is what takes a leader beyond success toward faithfulness.

## Types of Leaders

There are many types of leaders, all of whom may be very successful in their leadership activities. "Leaders vary in their values, their managerial styles, and their priorities. Some are primarily concerned with making a difference in society, others are concerned with being the best in their field."[1] Successful leadership involves mobilizing people to achieve a goal, or to reach a destination, or to make a difference in the larger organization or community.

Various types of leaders strive to lead their organizations in varied directions. For instance:

- Jealous leaders lead their organization to a place where other organizations already are. They strive to model other successful groups or organizations.
- Greedy leaders lead their group to a place where it can then serve them. They strive to add resources to the organization and then ensure that those resources are at their disposal.
- Frightened leaders lead their assembly to a place where only the most vocal want it to be. Those with the most power easily sway them.
- Opportunistic leaders lead their outfit to a place where it can only stay for a brief period of time. They are extremely selective in the indicators that they read and reveal to the public, hoping to move onto the next higher position of leadership before the overrated status of their current outfit is discovered.
- Naïve leaders lead their cluster to a place where they only perceive it to be. They become pawns led by others and are never able to grasp the big picture of what they are leading.
- Faithful leaders lead their congregation to a place where it can accomplish God's mission. Above all else, they strive to serve God.

Various types of successful leaders acquire similar sets of skills. Highly esteemed and highly despised leaders often use similar skills. Their aims and their methods, however, will differ greatly. Like other books on leadership, this book encourages the leaders to acquire and practice several skills in order to mobilize the people they are leading to make a difference. What this book does differently, however, is suggest how each of those skills may be used in a faithful manner, rather than merely in a successful manner.

I believe that there are several skills that are absolutely essential to leadership. Tasks such as envisioning, prioritizing, leading change, and mentoring, are all salient to one's success, no matter what type of leader one may be. The purpose of this book is to offer you faithful ways of carrying out the tasks of leadership.

# Faithfulness

Before detailing a process that you may use to fine-tune your leadership skills toward more faithful ends, I need to reveal a few of my assumptions about faithfulness. It will be difficult to embrace the characteristics of faithful leadership described in this book if some of the following assumptions about faithfulness are not also held or at least understood by the reader.

First of all, the way that I use the term *faithfulness* presumes a commitment to God. For Christians, it presumes a commitment to Jesus Christ. Before one can strive to serve God, one must believe that God exists, and even beyond that, the person must have made a commitment to following God. The ultimate aim of one's faithfulness should be directed toward God. Other forms of faithfulness are important, but secondary to being faithful to God.

A secondary category of faithfulness is a desire to accomplish God's will. This obviously assumes God *has* a will for our lives, and *if known,* assumes that we desire to strive for that end. Being faithful involves trusting God to do the right thing through us and around us. Paul expresses it this way: "For it is God who is at work in you enabling you both to will and to work for his good pleasure" (Philippians 2:13). God working in; people working out. That is the role of faithfulness.

This characteristic of faithfulness naturally leads to another presumed characteristic of faithfulness, namely that God is active in our lives today. Although faithful people may have various ideas about the degree of God's involvements and intersections with our lives, I hold an assumption that faithfulness, as an absolute minimum, presupposes God's ability to act in our lives today. My views of faithfulness assume that God is alive, desires to be in relationship with those who have made a commitment, and is able to act personally within the lives of those striving to be faithful.

# Leaders Are Grown

Not only do I bring assumptions to this book about what it means to be faithful, I bring assumptions about leadership that need to be disclosed before we begin. The primary assumption that I bring to the table is a belief that leaders are grown and not born. For the most part, leadership skills are developed rather than inherited. Some people possess certain natural characteristics of leadership, but even the natural traits must be developed in order to be workable. Well-known leadership expert Peter Drucker suggests that the lessons about whether or not leaders are born or made are unambiguous. "There may be 'born leaders,' but there surely are far too few of them to depend upon. Leadership must be learned and can be learned ... 'leadership personality,' 'leadership style,' and 'leadership traits' do not exist."[2] Drucker suggests that there are simply too many different styles of leadership to be able to point to one set of characteristics and claim that this set makes born leaders. We would be far better off to spend the time developing as leaders rather than spend it wondering whether or not we are "born leaders."

We need quality leaders today and quality does not come without focus and practice. "The dearth of leadership is apparent throughout society. No matter where we turn, we see a lack of faith in the leadership of our schools, religious organizations, and governments ... if Martians descended someplace in the United States and demanded that we take them to our leaders, we would have to think twice about where to take them."[3] We cannot assume that everyone in a church leadership position already possesses the gift of leadership. Quite the contrary! In a recent George Barna survey, he reports that only five percent of today's pastors possess the gift of leadership! "While 69% [of the pastors] claim that their primary gift is teaching or preaching, relatively few pastors—5%—say that they are gifted as leaders."[4] If you are one of the pastors who claims to have the gift of leadership and you still want to read this book and other books on leadership, congratulations on not taking your gift for granted! If you are a pastor or church leader who does not claim to have the gift of leadership, congratulations, this book can help! I believe that we should have lots of books on church leadership for pastors and other church leaders who are in the 95 percent category. I believe that many of the church's most faithful leaders of today are in the part of the group that does not claim to have the gift of leadership. There is little difference in potential for a leader with the gift of leadership and one without the gift. The tasks will merely come more easily for the former group than the latter.

I am convinced that any person can learn to be a leader and that any follower of God can learn to be a faithful leader. James M. Kouzes and Barry Z. Posner, in illustrating an unlikely candidate for leadership conclude that he, "is proof that you don't have to wait for someone else to lead, and you can lead without a title, a position, or a budget."[5] Every pastor and every church member, at some point, will be called upon to be a leader. How faithful will you be in your leadership role?

## Leadership Skills

In this book I will present the skills that I believe are absolutely essential for leaders to develop, namely, envisioning, attending to personal gifts, prioritizing, responding to crises, leading change, mentoring, caring for oneself, and asserting holistic leadership. I will show how each skill can be honed to become a faithful characteristic of leadership as opposed to merely a successful characteristic of leadership. Even though I present my essential list of leadership skills, this should not be the only book that you read on leadership. This is not a comprehensive book on leadership. There simply was not room in these pages to present various views of leadership or the full range of leadership skills required for today's leaders.

Other writers present alternate sets of essential characteristics for effective leadership. Stephen Covey's list includes pathfinding, aligning, and empowering.[6] Warren Bennis suggests that there are five things that board members require of their leaders, namely, technical competence, people skills, conceptual skills, judgment skills, and character.[7] James Bolt challenges leaders to embrace "the three dimensional framework … for the development of an individual's business, leadership, and personal effectiveness skills."[8] I assume that you have read other books on leadership prior to reading this one or that this will only be the first.

"Leadership is both complex and simple. It is an art and a science, it involves change and stability, it draws upon personal attributes and requires interpersonal relationships, it sets vision and results in action, it honors the past and exists for the future, … it is transformational and transactional, … it requires learning and unlearning, it centers on values and is seen in behaviors."[9] There certainly is a lot to learn about leadership, even more to learn about faithful leadership. With that in mind, we shouldn't waste any more time. Only one more section before we begin. I present a little about my background in order for you to understand the context of my thoughts.

# Background

My current context for ministry is that I serve as the executive minister for the American Baptist Churches of Ohio, a region consisting of over 290 congregations spread throughout most of Ohio. My primary duties include articulating a vision for the organization, overseeing staff, strengthening congregations, and encouraging joint mission work. I have made presentations regarding congregational life and health throughout the United States and Canada in a variety of denominational settings.

I began my present position in 1996. Previously, I held four different pastorates in a variety of settings. I have assumed that the primary audience for this book will be pastors of local congregations. Thus, I often refer to the context of ministry as a congregation. I recognize, however, that many laypersons, small-group leaders, committee leaders, and leaders of other types of organizations will choose to read this book. I encourage those whose primary context is not a local congregation to substitute whatever context may be more appropriate when the word *congregation* is encountered.

Finally, I never intend for anything that I write to be the "final answer" on a subject. I write for the same reasons that I read, namely to increase dialogue, dreams and discussion.

---

1   Richard Beckhard, *"On Future Leaders,"* in The Leader of the Future, *ed. Frances Hesselbein, Marshall Goldsmith, and Richard Beckard (San Francisco: Jossey-Bass Publishers, 1996), 128.*

2   Peter F. Drucker, *"Not Enough Generals Were Killed,"* in The Leader of the Future, *ed. Frances Hesselbein, Marshall Goldsmith, and Richard Beckard (San Francisco: Jossey-Bass Publishers, 1996), xi.*

3   James F. Bolt, *"Developing Three-Dimensional Leaders,"* in The Leader of the Future, *ed. Frances Hesselbein, Marshall Goldsmith, and Richard Beckard (San Francisco: Jossey-Bass Publishers, 1996), 163.*

4   George Barna, The Barna Report *(September/October 1997): 4.*

5   James M. Kouzes, & Barry Z. Posner, *"Seven Lessons for Leading the Voyage to the Future,"* in The Leader of the Future, *ed. Frances Hesselbein, Marshall Goldsmith, and Richard Beckard (San Francisco: Jossey-Bass Publishers, 1996), 109.*

6   Stephen Covey, *"Three Roles of the Leader in the New Paradigm,"* in The Leader of the Future, *ed. Frances Hesselbein, Marshall Goldsmith, and Richard Beckard (San Francisco: Jossey-Bass Publishers, 1996), 152–3.*

7   Warren Bennis, On Becoming a Leader *(Reading, Mass.: Addison-Wesley Publishing Company, 1989).*

8   *James F. Bolt, "Developing Three-Dimensional Leaders," in* The Leader of the Future, *ed. Frances Hesselbein, Marshall Goldsmith, and Richard Beckard (San Francisco: Jossey-Bass Publishers, 1996), 167.*

9   *Dave Ulrich, "Credibility x Capability," in* The Leader of the Future, *ed. Frances Hesselbein, Marshall Goldsmith, and Richard Beckard (San Francisco: Jossey-Bass Publishers, 1996), 210.*

# 1

## DISCERNING A VISION FROM GOD

**M**OST PASTORS ARE CONVINCED THAT A VISION is a good thing for a congregation to possess. Most pastors, however, underestimate the power of a strong vision. A vision can help new congregations focus and older congregations reenergize. A vision can turn surviving congregations into thriving congregations and maintenance organizations into movement organizations. A strong pastor can inspire a congregation to move forward. A strong vision can carry it all the way there.

What makes a strong vision? A strong vision is one that moves the congregation along. Developing a strong vision is similar to adding a "most valuable player" to your congregational team. The traditional definition of a "most valuable player" is one who helps every other teammate perform better. A strong vision will enhance every other aspect of your congregation.

What are the components of a strong vision and how is one developed? For a congregation, the key determinant for a strong vision is ensuring that its source is God. In fact, that is precisely what makes the process a Christian process. Any leader can envision, but a faithful leader discerns a vision from God. Discernment is the fundamental ingredient. Looking to God to supply a vision is the first and most important aspect of faithful envisioning. Below, you will find this and nine other aspects of discerning a strong vision for your congregation.

1

## Looking to God to Supply the Vision

Successful leaders create visions. Faithful leaders discern the vision from God. For congregations, visions come from God. "'For as the heavens are higher than the earth, so are my ways higher than your ways, and my thoughts than your thoughts'" (Isaiah 55:9). No one else knows better than God what your church needs to be doing. Faithful leaders begin the leadership task by asking God what is desired for the future of the congregation.

Never doubt God's ability to supply a vision for your congregation. God regularly supplies a cornucopia of needs for the church. God founded the church and not only wants it to continue, but to flourish. God energizes worship. God gifts people for service. God calls people to leadership. God plants new churches. God also supplies visions for ministries.

Often, the difference between surviving and thriving as a church is discerning a vision from God. Although it may appear to be implied, *thriving* is not about numbers. Numbers primarily belong in the realm of success rather than in the realm of faithfulness. Thriving is about doing the ministry that God has called us to do. There is no greater satisfaction for a church body than knowing that it is heading in a direction established by God. Faithful ministry is concerned with serving God, not the world.

The realization that the vision for your congregation must come from God brings with it both good and bad news. The good news is that the leader is freed from producing the vision. The bad news is that the leader is no longer in control of the timing and the nature of the vision. Discerning a vision from God is not always an easy process. It can occur during a stroll to Emmaus, or it can involve a forty-year trek in the wilderness. In either case, however, the processes used are the same. We discern a vision from God by using the channels already established by God for revealing information—namely prayer, Bible study, and reflection.

2

*A sample prayer meeting designed to discern a vision from God might be formatted as follows:*

 **Scripture reading (10 minutes)**
Read Psalm 86, 126, 127, Isaiah 40:17–24; 42:8–9; 43:18–21

 **Small-group discussion (20 minutes)**
- Ask, "For what are you thankful in our congregation's history?"
- Ask, "For what are you thankful in our congregation today?"
- Ask, "What needs exist among our members?"
- Ask, "What needs exist in our community?"

 **Prayer time (30 minutes)**
Prayers might be silent, conversational, or prepared, but ...
- Should include ample time for listening
- Each person should listen for God to reveal ideas about a vision for your church

 **Return to small groups (15 minutes)**
Share insights from silent prayer time

 **Small-group reporting (10 minutes)**

## Prayer

When is the last time that your congregation held a true prayer meeting for the purpose of asking God what you should be doing as a church? Many local church bylaws contain extensive sections detailing who can call a business meeting. Most often, this is an effort to

3

control the power associated with business meetings, but prayer meetings can be much more powerful than business meetings! However, bylaws often have little to say about who can call a prayer meeting. As a leader of your congregation, gather other leaders together for a time of discerning a vision from God through prayer. Spend time praising God for all that God already is doing in your midst, then ask God for a vision for the future. Remember, we have not because we ask not.

In your prayer meeting, be sure to give God equal speaking time. If you are going to seek God's vision through prayer, then your prayers must include ample time for God to reveal the vision to you. In discerning a vision through prayer, learn to listen to God in silence for at least as long as you express your ideas to God. Give God sufficient time to respond to your requests. I am amazed at how many people make a request to God yet never give God a chance to respond during the conversation. Prayer is conversation. God needs a chance to respond to our requests! The key to *all* good communication is to listen more than we talk. Thus, the key to good communication with God is to spend more time listening for answers and waiting for visions.

### Bible Study

A second way to discern God's vision is through Bible study. Examining God's writings is an excellent way to discern God's direction for the church today. The following types of passages all make great sources for discerning a vision:

- Kingdom of God passages
- Parables
- Names for God
- Names for the church
- Themes of particular epistles

Additionally, the following Scriptures may be helpful for discerning a vision:

- Matthew 6:19–21,33; 9:37–38;
- Mark 4:26–29; 8:1–10; 9:24;

- Luke 2:52; 5:36–37; 9:25; 22:27;
- John 4:34; 7:37–38;
- Acts 11:17–18; 28:30–31;
- Romans 8:6–8;
- 1 Corinthians 9:22–23; 10:31;
- 2 Corinthians 4:16–18.

New Testament Scriptures portray more than one local church. They describe the workings, the dynamics, and the struggles of many different congregations. The Corinthian church was shamed into working on their internal divisions. The church at Ephesus was challenged to strive for a unity that would become a model for all. The Philippian church was praised in an effort to erase their timidity over handling more serious matters. The Thessalonians were given hope to help them develop into a more mature church. Studying Scripture is an excellent tool for gaining a perspective on what God might be revealing to your congregation today.

### Reflection

Reflection is a third method of discerning a vision from God. God can use a multitude of formats, in addition to prayer and Scripture, to reveal future directions. Do you ever feel the power of God more dramatically in some worship services than others? God was probably trying to reveal something to you. Have you ever had an inclination to phone and see if someone is all right? God might have been urging you to make the call. Have you ever felt the intense presence of God while driving? When is the last time an idea flashed into your mind? God uses a variety of everyday occurrences to speak to us. Visions are often revealed in the midst of everyday life.

Scripture records a plethora of creative avenues used by God to reveal directions to people. Morton Kelsey states that 3,874 of the 7,957 verses in the New Testament refer to some manifestation of the Holy Spirit![1] At a recent meeting, the director of our international missions program suggested that one of the main differences between

*One method that some congregations have successfully used to discern a vision from God is to host an evening of small-group activities that incorporate both Bible study and reflection and can include other tools as well. This method assumes that the reader of this book also will draw together a leadership team to assist with the evening's activities.*

### ☞ Preparation:

Place the following headings on easy-to-read cards. (Categories may be added or deleted from the list.)
- Building upon our identity
- Old Testament passages
- New Testament passages
- Names for God and the church
- Arts and crafts
- Conversational prayer
- Silent reflection

### ☞ Group exercise

As each member of the leadership team is positioned in a different part of the room and holds up a card listing one of the titles above, ask each participant to walk toward one of the groups. Each group should be led by a team leader and be given forty-five minutes to ponder what God might be revealing to your church about a possible vision for your congregation. Use the particular heading as a backdrop for your discussion. The emphasis should be upon discernment. One of the team leaders should offer a prayer for wisdom from God prior to breaking into the small groups. A description of each sample group is given below:

### Building upon our identity

This group will be asked to discuss significant ideas pertaining to your local church identity. Is there something about your history, your theology, or your personality that might have a direct bearing upon God's vision for your immediate future?

### Old Testament passages

The leader of this group should read the following Old Testament passages in advance of the discernment night and choose several for the group to read and focus upon during its time together. Additional passages might be added. Is there a particular Old Testament Scripture that gives rise to a possible image for your congregation's vision?

- Genesis 32:24–32
- Leviticus 26:40–42
- Numbers 22:12–14
- Deuteronomy 26:16–19; 30:15–20
- Joshua 2:8–14; 3:5–7
- Judges 5:1–11
- 1 Samuel 3:1–11; 16:6–11
- 1 Kings 3:10–14; 19:9–16
- 2 Chronicles 20:3–19
- Psalms 24, 37, 42, 46, 73, 95, 122, 127, 133, 139
- Isaiah 28:20–21; 30:18–26; 35; 40:3–8,27–31; 43:18–21; 46:3–10; 58:6–12
- Jeremiah 31:30–33; 32:40–44
- Ezekiel 11:19–20; 20:20,41–48
- Hosea 14:5–7
- Joel 2:28–32
- Micah 6:6–8
- Zechariah 2:1–5; 4:1–10

### New Testament passages

The leader of this group should read the following New Testament passages in advance of the discernment night and choose several for the group to read and focus upon during its time together. Additional passages might be added. Is there a particular New Testament Scripture that gives rise to a possible image for your congregation's vision?

- Matthew 5:13–16; 6:19–21; 9:37–38; 11:28–30; 16:15–19; 18:19–20; 22:36–40; 24:14; 25:34–40; 28:18–20
- Mark 4:26–29; 8:1–10; 9:24; 10:43–45
- Luke 4:18–19,43–44; 5:36–37; 9:25
- John 4:23; 7:37–38; 10:14–18; 13:34–35; 20:21
- Acts 1:8; 2:41–47; 4:32–35; 6:1–7; 11:17–18; 28:30–31
- Romans 8:6–8; 12:1–8; 15:1–7
- 1 Corinthians 9:22–23; 12:12–31
- 2 Corinthians 4:16–18; 5:17–6:1
- Galatians 5:13–15; 6:1–2
- Ephesians 1:22–23; 2:19–22; 3:6,14–21; 4:11–16; 5:23–24
- Colossians 1:24–28; 3:15–16
- 1 Thessalonians 1:3; 5:11
- Hebrews 10:24–25; 13:7
- 1 Peter 2:9–10
- 1 John 1:5–7; 4:7–21

### Names for God and the church

The leader of this group should read the following names in advance of the discernment night and choose several for the group to focus upon during its time together. Additional names might be added. Is there a particular name for God or symbol of the church that gives rise to a possible image for your congregation's vision?

### Names for God

- God
- I Am
- Lord
- Eternal
- Living
- Holy One
- Mighty
- Heavenly
- Alpha and omega
- Ancient of days
- Anointed
- Author and perfecter of our faith
- Author of salvation
- Beloved
- Blessed and only sovereign
- Righteous Branch
- Bread of Life
- Bridegroom
- Bright morning star
- Carpenter
- Cornerstone
- Door
- Emmanuel
- Guardian of our souls
- Head
- Heir of all things
- High priest
- Horn of salvation
- Judge
- King
- Lamb
- Light of the world
- Lily of the valley
- Living stone
- Majestic
- Mediator
- Physician
- Propitiation
- Purifier and refiner
- Ransom
- Rock
- Root
- Savior
- Servant
- Shepherd
- Sower
- Teacher
- Truth
- Vine
- Way
- Word

### Names for the Church

- Believers
- Bethel
- Body of Christ
- Bride of Christ
- Building
- City of God
- Community
- Fellowship
- Flock
- Dwelling of God
- Household
- Kingdom
- Koinonia
- Mount Zion
- One Body
- People of God
- Spiritual House
- Temple

### Arts and crafts

The leader of this group should bring several craft items for this group to work with in discerning God's vision. The materials might include magazines, construction paper, modeling clay, markers, paints, scissors, etc. This group should work at creating an image of what they believe God wants their congregation to become.

### Conversational prayer

Some participants may prefer to gather for conversational prayer during this time. The leader of this group also should build in a time of listening and silence.

### Silent reflection

Some individuals may choose to sit alone during this portion of the meeting in order to listen to what God might be saying to them personally about the future vision of your congregation. Possible reflective topics might include:

- A time when you felt God's presence in a special way in a worship service
- A time when you were touched in a powerful way by a ministry, in the church or outside of it.

---

- A need you have that isn't being addressed through the church's ministry
- People you know who need to be touched by the power of God's transforming love
- What God wants you to be as a church

(These categories also could be used by the conversational prayer group.)

### ✄ *Reporting*

Ask each group to report and record the ideas on newsprint. The leadership team should listen for commonalties among the groups. The beginnings of a vision could surface during this part of the meeting.

---

the Christian church in the Western and Eastern hemispheres is the Eastern churches' reliance upon the Holy Spirit for daily direction. In this respect, the Western church has much to learn from the rest of the world. The Holy Spirit guides us, directs us, teaches us, and empowers us. As you reflect upon the future of your congregation, allow God's Spirit to reveal the future to you.

The process that a pastor uses to reflect upon his or her congregation is aimed at garnering the big picture of the congregation. Once the big picture is amassed, the faithful leader then trusts God to paint another picture of what the congregation might become in the future. Finally, the leader allows God to transform the present-day picture of the congregation into the futuristic picture of the congregation.

I regularly try to gain a balcony viewpoint of my organization in order to also gain a better perspective on what it might become. Ronald A. Heifetz speaks of "getting on the balcony" of your congregation in order to reflect upon its future.[2] Often, as my plane is leaving the state of Ohio to travel to another meeting, I begin to see my organization from a different perspective. I really don't think that's what Heifetz had in mind when he wrote of gaining a balcony perspective, but sometimes physical distance from an organization can provide needed emotional distance. The emotional distance can open up channels for God's revelation. Riding on a plane, taking a walk at a conference, or driving a car over undulating hills are some of the more frequent times that God has added to the picture of what my organization might become.

Never seek to limit a God as big as ours. Strive to discover God's vision for your congregation. Don't force God to hit you over the head with the vision as God did for Peter and Cornelius! Because of our obstinacy, sometimes God is forced to be both powerful and creative just to get a point across. Would Peter ever have said, "I truly understand that God shows no partiality" (Acts 10:34), if Cornelius had not received a congruent vision? In the midst of the congruent visions, while Peter is still preaching, the Holy Spirit falls upon the Gentile people. Indeed, God can be both creative and convincing! God may reveal the vision for your congregation to a group or to an individual. God may reveal the vision to a trustee, or God may reveal it to a custodian. As a leader, seek God's vision directly and listen for God's vision in the words of others, but most important, trust that God will supply the vision for your congregation.

God's vision for your church may come like a bolt of lightning, or it may come in the flicker of a candle, but God is the source of faithful visions. I challenge you to continue to ponder the vision for your congregation as you read further about characteristics of a strong vision.

## A Vision Pulls the Congregation to It

The second characteristic of faithful envisioning is that both leaders and followers in the congregation are pulled by the visions that originate with God. Successful leaders simply push the plans. When envisioning plans go awry, many leaders naturally become frustrated because the plans are the locus of attention rather than a means to achieve a vision. "In many failed transformations, you find plans and programs trying to play the role of vision."[3] For the faithful leader, the vision provides the focus. A faithful leader trusts that the vision discerned from God will eventually pull the congregation to it.

Imagine kicking a rock down the street. When you come to a curb or other obstacle, it is decision time for the one kicking the rock. If the rock, however, is made of iron and is being pulled by a magnet, then the magnet will pull the rock around any obstacle encountered, provided that the magnet has enough power. That is the difference between pushing your own plans and following a vision from God. Visions from God contain enough power to maneuver around any human or physical obstacle encountered in this world. Others think of visions as strings. It is much easier to pull a piece of string than it is to push it forward.

The cloud of God, mentioned in the ninth chapter of Numbers and elsewhere, provides an excellent illustration of the way God directs and pulls people. God used a cloud by day and a pillar of fire by night to lead the Israelites through the wilderness. Whenever the cloud moved, the people moved. Whenever the cloud rested, the people rested. The people abided with the cloud and with the fire. Whether the cloud remained for a day, a week, a month, or longer, the people remained, trusting that the cloud eventually would move again.

I wonder if we would be that patient today. Can you imagine the murmurings that might emit from one of today's congregations if the cloud remained in one spot for longer than a month or two? "I just know we missed it!" someone might suggest. "Yes, I definitely think that this cloud looks different," another might add as a comment of confirmation. People in more traditional congregations might express disdain for the frequency of the moves. "We've only been here one night. I like this spot. Let's stay awhile. Surely, the cloud will come around again." Such confrontations could easily lead to a vote. Such votes could easily lead to a split. Such splits, although common in our culture, did not seem to be a part of the Israelite picture. For all of their struggles in the wilderness, at least the Israelites sojourned together. Successful leaders have a need to be in front. Faithful leaders have a need to follow God.

In the analogy of the cloud and fire, it is important to note that in Exodus 14:19, the cloud even came around behind the Israelites and protected them from the Egyptians. A vision from God can guide the congregation into new directions. It also can protect the congregation from its past. A congregation seeking to follow God's vision must always remember to look up before looking forward.

I believe that following a vision from God provides the only realistic means for a congregation to move forward together. When applying this concept, faithful leaders will not actually lead. Faithful leaders will follow God's vision. Others will follow the leaders, trusting in God's faithfulness.

In this scenario of leadership, the burden is not upon the leaders; it is upon the vision. That realization should provide comfort to many leaders. Faithful leaders become followers of the vision. Others follow leaders who are following the vision. "More than ever before in history, the answer lies in following our vision and purpose, following our principles for managing toward that purpose, and following all the people who will make an organization's vision happen."[4]

## *Faithful Leaders Must Articulate the Vision*

The third characteristic of building a vision that will work for your congregation is for the leaders to consistently and clearly articulate the vision. But, in order to articulate the vision, the leaders must be firmly committed to it. Rick Warren holds a monthly "SALT" meeting with his leadership team in which they renew their commitment to the vision. Warren demonstrates his commitment to this meeting over all others, "If I'm feeling ill, I do not hesitate giving up speaking to the 10,000 in the crowd, but I have to be dying to miss being with the core at SALT. It is my opportunity to reemphasize the privilege of serving Christ."[5]

I contend that what attracts us most to a strong vision is not so much the content of the vision, but rather the leader's commitment to the vision. Visions that work for us are visions that work for our leaders. The fact that the vision never ceases to motivate its leaders is what compels others to follow the leaders. Leaders who use the model of producing their own vision feel a burden to produce a flashy vision that has motivation power. Faithful leaders commit to a vision because it comes from God, not because it is flashy. In terms of motivation, the content of the vision is secondary to the commitment to it demonstrated by faithful leaders. Peter Drucker suggests, "Everyone must be able to provide input and at least buy into the vision and direction. Once people know where they are going, top managers cannot divorce themselves from the implementation process. All must be facilitators and cheerleaders."[6] Successful leaders enjoy being at the top. Faithful leaders play whatever role is necessary in order to advance the vision.

Once a commitment is made to the vision, a leader must emphasize the vision at every turn. Pastors must speak of the vision often in sermons, Bible studies, new-member classes, conversations, newsletter articles, and bulletins. Committee and group leaders must articulate the vision for their group at every meeting. Moderators and session leaders must find ways to bring the vision into business meetings. Guests need to encounter the vision during their first visit to your congregation through print media, through the worship service, in the welcoming spirit, and in the ethos of the congregation. If the leader is not committed to the vision, the promotion will become onerous. For the faithful leader committed to the God-supplied vision, all of the promotion will come naturally.

Nearly anyone who excels at a task has a way of making the task look easy. The secret to making leadership look easy is to put the burden upon the vision rather than yourself. In any congregation, the burden should not be upon the leader but rather upon the vision. "'Take my yoke upon you, and learn from me,'" God declared (Matthew 11:29). The primary responsibility of a leader is not to make sure that everyone in the congregation is carrying out his or her list of goals. The primary responsibility of a leader is to lift a vision to such a height that anyone who looks up can see it. "Write the vision; make it plain on tablets, so that a runner may read it. For there is still a vision for the appointed time; it speaks of the end, and does not lie. If it seems to tarry, wait for it; it will surely come, it will not delay" (Habakkuk 2:2–3). Habakkuk was told to write the message in such a manner that even those running by might see it. That is the task of faithful leaders, to lift up the vision so high, that even those with the busiest of schedules can still see the vision.

## The Vision Will Attract Others

The more a vision is articulated, the more it will attract others to it. This fourth component of developing a vision for your congregation is more passive than active. The passiveness of this component differs greatly between successful leaders and faithful leaders. Successful leaders feel the need to constantly build ownership of the vision. They convince, conjole, and sometimes connive others to join their cause. Faithful leaders, on the other hand, use this phase of the envisioning process as a test to ensure that the vision came from God. If God supplied the vision, it will indeed attract others to it. God by nature is contagious. Thus, God's visions will naturally attract others to them.

Faithful leaders spend more time lifting up a vision and less time trying to figure out how to motivate others. People are warmed watching leaders commit to a vision. People are skeptical of efforts made to manipulate them. The first task of a faithful leader is to lift up the vision. Individual task assignments and job descriptions are always secondary to lifting up the vision for the group. Most people can devise better ways of making their own contributions toward the accomplishment of the vision, once they see that the leaders have committed to a vision produced by God. There is a place for individual goals, but ensuring that they are carried out to the letter is not the primary responsibility of a faithful leader. Many leaders feel a burden to motivate others. Faithful leaders are so captivated by a vision that they cannot help but point others toward the same vision.

I truly believe that a vision's ability to attract others is part of the evidence that it has come from God. This can be a sensitive area. I am aware that many authors have suggested (and supported their suggestions biblically) that conflict is a natural part of leadership. I agree to an extent. Visions create change and changes create conflicts. Not everyone in a congregation may be able to "buy into" a new vision for their congregation, even God's vision for the congregation. But, there is a Chinese Proverb that suggests, "He who thinketh he leadeth and hath no one following is only taking a walk." As long as a critical mass opposes the vision, it is time for vision adjustment rather than vision advancement. Even in vision advancement, the major component will be listening rather than convincing. The initial decision of whether or not a vision is from God lies with those who received the vision and those who are charged with leadership. But we must remember that God ultimately wants to get things done, not just create dissonance. In a very short time, Jesus found twelve people who would fully commit to his vision and a host of others whose hearts committed before their feet followed. A vision that comes from God will eventually attract others to it.

## Visions Are Easily Communicated

Simplicity is the fifth component to a vision that works. In order to demonstrate that a vision need not be complicated in order to work, I will introduce an example from a Broadway performance *Les Miserables*. The powerful music of *Les Miserables* is eclipsed only by its storyline.

Victor Hugo paints the life of Jean Valjean, a man who has had only the worst of times until age forty-seven.[7] The first chapter of Jean's life is both lengthy and laden with difficulty. He is imprisoned for stealing a loaf of bread for his six hungry siblings. Reaching through a window to secure a meal was the modus operandi. Because there were people upstairs in the house that enticed Jean with its freshly baked bread, the jail sentence carried with it a lengthy duration of five years. Four escape attempts transformed five into nineteen.

Jean quickly discovers that release from one's environment is not enough to turn bad days into good or bad nature into good. Emotionally and physically tagged an ex-convict, Jean discovers that the *convict* part of his plight carries more weight than the ex- in front of the convict. His new label bars even the necessities of life from being purchased with money. Jean finds himself useless, necessityless, hopeless, and visionless. New life, however, is just around the corner. The source of new life often is the most surprising part of a good story. In this case, new life comes in the form of a nameless bishop.

Never underestimate the nameless. The Bible is full of nameless heroes and heroines: the repentant thief, the Syrophoneacian woman, the rich man and Lazarus, the woman at the well, the man who carried the cross. Possibly they are nameless because their vision is more substantive than their name.

In *Les Miserables,* help comes from the nameless bishop who befriends Jean Valjean. The nameless bishop in turn allows the traveler to remain anonymous. The bishop speaks, "You need not tell me who you are. This is not my house; it is the house of Christ. It does not ask any comer whether he has a name, but whether he has an affliction."[8]

Overcome with emotion but not gratitude, Jean recognizes that the silver plates from which he eats represent more money than he has ever seen in his life. Before dawn, he departs the bishop's home with silver plates in hand. Just as release from an old environment is not enough to turn bad days into good, or bad nature into good, neither is the mere presence of a new environment enough. The authorities confront Jean. With glee they discover the silver plates. With even more glee they drag him back to the bishop's house for an affidavit of the crime.

The bishop speaks, "Ah, there you are. You must have returned because you forgot these candlesticks, silver like the rest, also a gift like the rest." With much less glee and much more disdain, the authorities depart. Additional words are spoken to Jean alone, "Here are the candlesticks. You belong no longer to evil, but to good. Never forget that you have promised me to use this silver to become an honest man."⁹ Jean receives a gift. More important he receives a vision, "to become an honest man." Jean turns a deaf ear toward success and an open eye toward being faithful. Time and time again he chooses faithfulness and honesty over worldly success.

God's visions are seldom complicated. Jean's vision simply to "become an honest man" has stood the test of time for author Victor Hugo. It stills compels, drives, and delivers for those who witness the performances. Likewise, God's visions often are simple. "I give you ten commandments." Later, the ten were simplified even more to just two. Finally, we were left with *the* great commandment and *the* great commission. God, who certainly knows how to keep things simple, will probably present your congregation with a simple vision as well.

Visions need not be complicated. In fact, the more uncomplicated the vision, the more lucidly it can be communicated. There is no doubt what "becoming an honest man" means. Its clarity enhances its contagiousness. Although they come from business rather than the church, the following examples, cited by John Kotter, are excellent samples of easily communicated visions, "We are going to throw out some of the rule books and give employees more discretion to do the right thing for our customers," and, "We need to become less like an elephant and more like a customer-friendly *Tyrannosaurus rex*."¹⁰

Lest the process of faithful envisioning is sounding too simple, I deliver a warning. Surface simplicity does not always equate to simplicity beneath the surface. Although visions should be easily communicated, what goes on behind the vision in order to accomplish it may indeed be very complicated. I am not mechanically inclined. I have no idea what transpires behind the scenes when I push the accelerator, or when I listen to surround sound, or when I touch the keypad of a computer. I am largely ignorant of the how-to of modern conveniences. In my current position, I no longer live in a parsonage or manse. This has its obvious advantages. There are other days, however, when my family really misses the board of trustees, the caretakers of previous parsonages. If there was a leaky pipe before, my wife might call the board of trustees, informing them, "There is a leak in the sink, Jeff said that he would take a look at it." The reply would usually sound something like this, "Now there's no need to threaten us, ma'am, we will be there just as soon as we can. Tell your husband to lay hands on the sick today, but don't touch that sink!" I seldom worry about what goes on behind the light switch when I turn it on, and could do little about it even if I did care, but I do appreciate its surface simplicity. When we are observing a congregation, we do not always care about what goes on behind the scenes to accomplish their vision. We do, however, want to know what their vision is.

That "vision thing," someone once called it. Publicly confessing one's lack of commitment to a vision can be the demise of any leader, even the president of the United States. The good news is that vision thing need not be complicated in order to work. I am convinced, however, that a strong leader must have a strong commitment to a vision in order to lead effectively.

## A Vision Will Inform

A simple vision has the power to inform decision making. That is the sixth characteristic of a vision that works. If you have to refer to a piece of paper to recall the vision, it will not inform your daily decision making. Faithful leaders should have in mind the vision of the congregation during every phone call, every piece of correspondence, every strategic effort to solve a problem, etc. The vision for the congregation that you are leading should inform both short- and long-term decision making. Not a day should go by where you cannot point to at least one decision or event influenced by the vision of your congregation.

The current vision for the organization that I lead is to make every task a ministry task. That vision has informed the development of our web page, the agendas of our board meetings, the design of our annual gatherings, the calling of staff, and the development of job descriptions. Bill Hudnut, former mayor of Indianapolis, wrote in his book, *Minister/Mayor,* "My father used to tell us that the essence of our education would be what we remembered after we had forgotten what we were taught."[11] That's the vision portion of the educational process. Once a vision becomes embedded in our minds, it can inform decisions insentiently.

In a former congregation, I remember a farmer constantly saying, "You are either expanding or declining; you never stay the same. Farming means growing." That philosophy informed all of his decision making. As a grain-elevator operator in the midst of a low-price crisis, he had a meeting with his creditors, who were concerned about his heavy debt. They were encouraging him to stop buying more grain and to start selling some of what he had.

At the close of the meeting, the creditors said, "Well, at least you're going to pick up the tab for the coffee today, aren't you?"

Bill replied, "If I had money for the coffee today, I'd buy more grain!" His vision never ceased informing his decision making. On another occasion, Bill received a contract from the government to store grain. Rather than build another elevator in which to store the grain, which might not be long-lived, he built a warehouse. When the government contracts ended, he sold the warehouse to a manufacturer. Bill always looked for ways to implement his vision. That's what leaders do.

In order to determine the extent to which your vision has influenced the members of your congregation, conduct a vision audit. Poll several members of your congregation, asking them their perceptions of the vision of your congregation. The answers will either tell you where to place more emphasis, or they may tell that it is time to move on to the next vision! If your current vision has been in place for several years and is no longer informing either your decision making as a leader or your followers' decisions to follow, it is time for a new vision.

## Mottoes Can Help Communicate Visions

A motto is a simple statement that helps describe a vision. Mottoes are the seventh component of working visions. A motto is a window to a vision. Mottoes are helpful because they provide pathways to the images behind them. Mottoes are even more easily communicated than visions. The vision for our organization, the American Baptist Churches of Ohio, is to make every task a ministry task. Our motto, adapted from Detroit, is "Ministry is job #1." The motto is a window to our vision.

A good motto should provide a strong indication of the content of the vision that lies behind it. It is both fun and educational to try to guess the visions behind advertising mottoes. The current motto for Hertz is, "Not exactly." Might their vision be "to precisely meet the needs of our customers"? The current motto for Avis is, "We try harder." Might their vision be "to envision every single Avis employee working harder than every single Hertz employee"? "No surprises" is the current motto for Holiday Inn. Might their vision be "to picture every traveler entering a Holiday Inn knowing exactly what to expect and where to find everything"? Their motto might also be slamming those other chains who have been purchasing other motels and placing their own logos out front. A historic hallmark for Holiday Inns has been to build their own buildings from the ground up.

Several congregations in our region have developed mottoes for their visions. One of the churches, known for its ability to produce mature, intellectual Christians, but desiring now to be more involved in the community, adopted the motto "The Growing Place." Another of our congregations, striving to impact their community through economic development, the adopt-a-block program, and new housing, adopted the motto "Building a Faith that Works." One congregation desiring to portray their long-standing emphasis upon the Holy Spirit adopted the motto "Enlivened by the Spirit of God ... Upward, Inward, Outward." In order to emphasize ministry, one of our congregations adopted the motto, "A Ministry for All People and All People for Ministry." "Come Close to God" is yet another's motto. Can you guess the visions behind these mottoes?

As an exercise, try to think of a motto for a congregation desiring to make every major decision through the discernment process as opposed to the democratic process. Try to think of a motto for a new church start that is desiring to understand a particular ethnic or cultural group and striving to meet their needs. Attempt these and other examples in order to practice forming mottoes. If God already has supplied a vision for your congregation, try to develop a motto as a window to it. A motto can greatly enhance the communication phase of the envisioning process.

## A Vision Is Not a Mission Statement

A vision differs from a mission statement. A vision is a short-term picture of where God would like your congregation to be in the next few years. A mission statement answers the long-term question as to why you exist. Unlike your vision, your mission statement probably will not change dramatically over the years. A mission statement is part of a congregation's identity. More specifically, the identity for a congregation is comprised of the organization's history, theology, and personality. A mission statement is part of the theological component of a congregation's identity. A mission statement reveals the major purposes for your congregation.

Developing a mission statement for a congregation is a wonderful exercise. Expecting a mission statement to become the prime motivator for your congregation is disaster. Mission statements simply do not contain enough specificity to provide direction for either the leaders or the followers of a congregation.

Many congregations spend huge amounts of time and energy producing mission statements. If the expectations from the mission statement are realistic, such effort is time well spent. Asking a group of people to reflect upon the purposes of your congregation can be a fruitful task. It often is helpful for congregations to spend time reflecting upon their entire identity, including their mission. Such information is invaluable to the envisioning process. A vision for any congregation must build upon its existing identity. In fact, the members of a congregation will not usually give permission to the leadership to pursue a new direction or a new vision until the leadership has demonstrated a sufficient understanding of the current identity of the congregation.[12]

The problem with mission-statement development usually occurs after the mission statement has been developed. Once a great deal of effort has been expended and a product has been produced in the form of a mission statement, people often expect the mission statement to motivate the members of the congregation. The problem is that most mission statements contain too much verbiage and too little uniqueness to provide any sense of direction for the congregation. The reason that your congregation exists may not be that different from similar congregations nearby. How your congregation chooses to accomplish that mission and where God wants your congregation to be in the short term, however, may be very different from the congregation across the street. In order to provide direction, specificity is needed. Mission statements are aimed at justifying one's existence. Visions are aimed at accomplishing that mission in unique ways.

# There Are Multiple Ways of Reaching a Vision

Because the vision comes from God and thus pulls the congregation to it, there are multiple ways of reaching the vision. The only surety is the fact that the congregation will reach the destination God has in mind. The pathways to a vision are totally unpredictable.

With a good vision, you don't have to know where each stone is in the water in order to reach the other side. Of course you may not end up at the precise spot on the other side that you had imagined, but you will reach the destination. Have you ever watched a raindrop flow down a window? Have you ever doubted that it would reach the bottom? Yet just as you can predict that the raindrop will reach the bottom of a pane, you can be sure that the pathway of the raindrop cannot be predicted. The destination is inevitable. The pathway is chaotic. One is totally predictable, the other totally unpredictable. In following a vision from God, the only reliable predictions lie with the destination, not the routes.

Thus, it is important not to become overly focused upon the means to a vision. For a faithful leader, a vision is a picture of the way things should be. Not what might be or what could be, but what should be. For faithful leaders, words like *possible* and *feasible* never touch the landscape of a vision, for such words relate to means and not ends. During the course of a vision, and especially at its genesis, obstacles seldom enter into the picture, not because the leader believes courageously that any obstacle can be overcome, but simply because they are not the focus at the moment. In the early stages, the leader is clueless as to means. The means may be simple. The means may be ludicrous. But the genesis of a vision is not the time for considering means.

Before considering means, a faithful leader must first be consumed by a vision. One cannot contemplate maneuvering through a pathway of obstacles until the destination has consumed the traveler. There will be no energy to overcome obstacles until the vision has been named worthy. Once the destination has come into focus, a multitude of means

25

will surface. Only those with fuzzy destinations complain of arduous avenues. People with clear visions never complain about means, because their focus is upon the ends. Once a leader has been proven faithful by being patient enough to let God supply the ends, continuing to let God supply the means to the ends is an easier task of faithfulness. Faithful leaders trust God to supply the means that lead to the ends.

This does not mean that faithful leaders do not try things, or that they sit back and wait upon God to *work* the means. On the contrary, faithful leaders try many different means to reach the ends. A faithful leader is constantly brainstorming ways to advance the vision. A faithful leader, however, never becomes overly discouraged when a particular set of means fails. The reason for the confidence is that the faithful truly believe God has supplied the vision. Only leaders who supply their own visions doubt the vision when the means fail. The faithful leader's response to catastrophe becomes, "OK, God, that path obviously did not work. What would you like me to try next to reach *your* vision for our congregation?" James must have trusted this characteristic of visions completely. "My brothers and sisters, whenever you face trials of any kind, consider it nothing but joy, because you know that the testing of your faith produces endurance; and let endurance have its full effect, so that you may be mature and complete, lacking in nothing" (James 1:2–4). When trials come, a faithful leader trusts that God will soon supply another course of action.

## Visions Can Change

The final component to building a faithful vision is recognizing that visions can change. Because a vision is a short-term picture of where God would like to take your congregation during the next few years, it obviously can change. The Spirit of God is just as willing to supply the next direction as the last direction. The Spirit of God would not allow Paul and his companions to enter Bithynia (Acts 16:6–10). The Spirit of God sent Barnabas and Mark in a different direction than Paul and Silas (Acts 15:37–41). The discernment process cannot cease once the vision has been supplied. Leaders must become like little children on a journey to their vacation destination, constantly asking God, "Are we there yet?" The leader should know when the destination has been reached, but in the process of getting there, proximity to the destination and direction of travel are sometimes less clear, prompting the need for consistent inquiry.

Our organization will never reach the point of having *every* task performed as a ministry. But knowing when the impact of the ministry vision has run its course will be a part of the discernment process. Then, we will trust God to supply the next chapter for the organization, by supplying the next short-term vision. God will supply not just one vision for your local group or congregation, but rather a series of visions. The faithful leader not only looks to God to supply the current vision, this type of leader looks to God to supply the next vision.

We must constantly strive to stay oriented toward God to both supply our vision and guide our means. "To orient oneself originally means to turn in the right direction. The noun *orient* originally meant the direction of the rising sun."[13] Discerning a vision is about looking in the right direction. Faithful leaders always look up before looking forward. Faithful leaders trust God to supply the vision for their congregation. Then they faithfully work toward achieving that vision until the next revelation is as clear as the preceeding one.

---

1   Morton Kelsey, Encounter with God *(Minneapolis: Bethany House, 1972).*

2   *Ronald A. Heifetz,* Leadership Without Easy Answers *(Cambridge, Mass.: The Belknap Press of Harvard University, 1994), 252.*

3   *John Kotter,* Leading Change *(Boston: Harvard Business School Press, 1996), 8.*

4   *Douglas K. Smith, "The Following Part of Leading," in* The Leader of the Future, *ed. Frances Hesselbein, Marshall Goldsmith, and Richard Beckard (San Francisco: Jossey-Bass Publishers, 1996), 200.*

5   *Rick Warren,* The Purpose Driven Church: Growth without Compromising Your Message and Mission *(Grand Rapids, Mich.: Zondervan Publishing Company, 1995), 392.*

6   *Drucker, "Not Enough Generals," xii.*

7   *Victor Hugo,* Les Miserables, *trans. Charles E. Wilbour (New York: Fawcett Premier, 1961).*

8   *Ibid., 19.*

9   *Ibid., 33.*

10  *Kotter, 91–92.*

11  *William H. Hudnut,* Minister/Mayor *(Philadelphia: The Westminster Press, 1987), 84.*

12  *For more information on understanding the identity of your organization, see C. Jeff Woods,* User Friendly Evaluation *(Bethesda, Md.: The Alban Institute, 1995), especially chapter two.*

13  *Loyd W. Allen,* Crossroads in Christian Growth *(Nashville: Broadman Press, 1989), 15.*

# ATTENDING TO AND REKINDLING OUR GIFTS

I N THE FIRST EPISTLE TO TIMOTHY, TIMOTHY RECEIVES these words, "Do not neglect the gift that is in you, which was given to you through prophecy with the laying on of hands by the council of elders" (1 Timothy 4:14). What gift? What prophecy? What council of elders? The reader is not informed of such details. All we know for sure is that Timothy must have neglected the gift, because we find these words in the second letter to Timothy, "I remind you to rekindle the gift of God that is within you through the laying on of my hands" (2 Timothy 1:6).

In the first letter, Timothy was encouraged not to neglect the gift that he received. At the onset of receiving the gift, it was aflame with possibilities. In the first set of instructions, Timothy is requested to attend to the gift within. Had he done that, he would not have faced the more difficult task of rekindling the gift. All that is required to keep a fire going is not to neglect it. Add another log as needed. Rearrange when necessary. Occasionally glance at it. Indeed, the greater task for a raging fire is controlling it, not keeping it going!

Whatever the gift, Timothy neglected it. We know that he failed to attend to his gift, for he was challenged to rekindle it later on. The writer makes it clear that the same gift is being alluded to in both letters because Timothy is told twice that this is the gift received through the laying on of hands. Only the second time, Timothy also is reminded that not only were the elders present, but so was the author! I suspect that had the author been speaking to Timothy in person, the conversation might have sounded something like this: "Remember now. I laid my own hands on you. I know you have this gift. You were commissioned because of it! Where is it? It is not evident within your leadership decisions. Rekindle it and get on with ministry."

Like Timothy, God asks many Christian leaders to rekindle their gifts. God often plants the spark of a call to ministry or a call to Christian leadership in someone at a very young age. Some respond immediately. Others try their hands at a number of vocations before settling down to rekindle the spark originally planted by God years before. It is not important whether you are setting out to attend to a fresh gift planted in your life by God or are aiming at rekindling a gift planted long ago. The important matter is that you are striving to be faithful in this moment. Your faithfulness in responding to God's call to Christian leadership brought you to this book. Read on to discover how to faithfully attend to or rekindle the gift that God has given you.

In the last chapter, the most important item to remember about visions was, "God will supply the vision for your congregation." The most important item to remember in this chapter is, "God will supply the gifts and the means to reach your vision." If at this point in your reading of this book, you already have discovered a vision from God for your congregation, learn to trust that vision. Learn to trust God to supply the gifts and the means to get you there. Trusting God does not cease when the vision comes. That is merely the beginning of the leader's reliable relationship with God. As you pursue your vision, don't become too anxious about process. The more we develop as faithful leaders, the more we learn to say, "He [God] must increase, but I must decrease" (John 3:30). Successful leaders do everything they can to advance the vision of the congregation. Faithful leaders put their entire trust in God to reach the vision supplied by God.

As we will see, trusting God does not constitute idleness. Just as discernment carries with it an active role for the vision recipient, so do attending to and rekindling the gifts of God. Faithful leaders pray, ask, and trust God to supply the gifts to reach the vision. They also work hard at attending to those gifts and even rekindling them when necessary.

We are challenged to attend to our gifts. We cannot neglect the gifts given to us by God. We should attend to them so that rekindling will not be necessary. Imagine that your gift from God is actually a fire flaming within your soul. Attending to that fire will require some work. What type of wood will you add to the fire? How will you contain it? Who else should be closest to the fire? Which peats can survive at a greater distance from the center? How hot should you let it get? How much heat is necessary to keep warm? In what direction is the wind blowing? How can you maximize the wind to fuel the fire? Which logs should be closest to the wind? Attending to a fire requires consistent and deliberate attentiveness.

## Listening for the Voice from Within

As I approached the summer between college and seminary, I knew that I needed a summer job. As I was strolling through the halls of Purdue University I came upon a summer job fair. The room was filled with displays of camps and conference centers. As I browsed the displays, the pictures from one of the displays captured my attention and captivated my interest. Clay tennis courts, Sea Ray ski boats, lighted baseball diamonds … it sounded too good to be true. Five seconds later I was interviewing. Five weeks later I was headed toward a camp in New Hampshire on beautiful Lake Winnepesaukee. My duties included instruction in baseball, water-skiing, and drama, and twenty-four-hour counseling to eight eight-year-olds for eight weeks. To me, eight was the perfect age, directly between wanting diapers changed and wanting girls. Eight seemed ideal. When one is eighteen, "ideal" can cover an extremely short span of time.

Once at camp, I had a wonderful four days. On the fifth day, the first camper arrived, dramatically altering my thoughts of the ideal age for campers. Mario was the first camper's name. Mario knew only two English expressions, "tennis" and "speed limit." I learned that his favorite sport was tennis and that his father kept complaining about the speed limits. The next camper spoke fluent English. I think he knew more English words than I did! He arrived with a sealed, stapled note from his parents, reading, "He's a spoiled fourth child and learns fast. Do what you can." The next camper came with a severe case of homesickness. Each camper came with his own particular set of needs and wants, all of which I was ill prepared to meet.

At the end of the second week of camp the camp director asked me if I wanted to lead an all-day fishing expedition. I asked if it was with my kids. He said, "No." And I replied, "I'd love to go." As I left with my new group of campers the next morning, my kids left for an overnight excursion on the island. I wouldn't see them for almost twenty-four hours. "What a welcome day off," I thought.

The five ten-year-olds in my boat fished for everything from flying fish to guppies. Within five minutes, Adam caught the first keeper.

"Quick, take it off the hook."

"I think it's time for you boys to take your own fish off the hooks."

"Don't you know how?"

I had to get another smart kid. All morning, they caught fish and I took them off the hooks. By noon everyone except Joel had caught something. Joel disliked being left out of the big catch. Just then, lightning flashed across the lake. Like dominoes, the boys began to cry. One yelled, "The boat is filling up with water."

"Wait a minute, it's not raining yet. Joel, what are you doing with that boat plug in your hand?"

"My hook caught in it."

"Put it back."

"I can't. The water's coming in too fast."

Only somewhat less dramatically than the sinking of the Titanic, we went down. Soon after that, the rains came, but you can only drip so much while in the water. Within minutes, we all were safely on shore, eating the only floatable item on our lunch menu, oranges.

On the return trip home, the boys were splashing one another with water. I figured, "What's the harm? They couldn't get any wetter." One of the oars hit me in the eye, causing it to bleed. Comforting consolations from ten-year-olds followed.

"He's going to die!"

"He'll lose his eye!"

"He'll go blind. We'll be stuck out here forever."

Back at camp, the kids told everyone what it feels like to escape death twice in one day. They didn't know it was actually three.

The director came into my bunk and suggested, "Your boys are over on the island. It's a shame you have to miss the overnight with them. After dinner, I'll point out to you where they are on the island, and you can row over to them."

"Sir, that's OK. Really. I don't mind staying here tonight. It might do them good to have a change of leadership for the night." I lost the argument. After dinner I started rowing over to the island with a sick feeling in my stomach. It was not from dinner. All I could think about was how nice it would have been to be away from them for just one night. I really needed it. After all, I had come for the sports facilities, not these kids. I barely had a chance to enjoy the sports equipment before the kids arrived. I was not in the mood to see any more kids. I was not in the mood to discipline. I was not in the mood to … My thoughts were broken by a noise coming from the island. Someone was chanting a word. I couldn't tell what it was. I rowed with more vigor. It sounded like a name. It sounded like my name. Someone was chanting my nickname!

"Woodsy, Woodsy, Woodsy," the boys chanted. Suddenly, I couldn't wait to see them. Like a batter rounding the base and heading for home, my boat kissed the beach. The boys hurled themselves into my boat.

"We missed you. We're playing pirates and we want you to be the head pirate!" That night, I played head pirate as I never had before. At that moment, I knew who was callin' my name.

Sometimes a series of catastrophes can cause us to focus upon our role more clearly. If God has called us to a particular role or a particular ministry, God will work with us until we are firmly planted upon the correct path. If God has called us into ministry as pastors, teachers, or leaders, we can trust that God will continue to call our names all the way to shore. "For the gifts and the calling of God are irrevocable" (Romans 11:29).

Inside each of us is a call that beckons. Inside each of us is a call constantly challenging us to rekindle the gift within. Leonard Sweet writes, "As Christians, we should be an echo of God's voice … Martin Luther insisted that God is a *Deus loquens*—a 'speaking God.'"[1] God not only speaks to us through events and people, God speaks to each of us from within ourselves. In that summer on Lake Winnepesaukee, I had been listening to the call of the sports facilities. In the moment that my boat reached the beach, I began listening to the call of the boys. I learned who was callin' my name. In that moment, I ceased being a consumer, and commenced being a leader for my group. I could have had a very successful summer by enjoying the sports facilities. I could not, however, have been faithful unless I put the needs of the boys ahead of my own.

## Discovering Your One Main Gift

The voice that calls from within takes us much more deeply into God's will than the experiences of just one summer. Inside is a call challenging us to attend to *the* gift, the gift of a lifetime. I am now convinced that each of us possesses a primary gift within us to attend to and rekindle. Although we experience many gifts throughout our

# How-to Section

*Tools for Discovery*

*Schedule a personal retreat in order to begin the process of discovering your one main gift from God. You may choose to retreat with a partner who has a similar goal or you may choose to retreat alone. The retreat might include the following components processed according to your own style and time available.*

 **Scripture reading**
- Genesis 1
- Ezra, Nehemiah, or Ruth
- 1 Kings 17–19
- Psalm 139
- Isaiah 40
- Micah
- Luke 4
- John 15–16
- Romans 12
- Hebrews 11

 **Devotional reading**
- Bring along your own set of favorite passages or books.
- As you read, reflect upon why these are your favorites.

 **Journal exercises**
- List the five most recent events that have produced a high level of satisfaction.
- What do these events have in common?

**Prayer**
- Spend time thanking God for all of the gifts that you have received.
- Ask God to reveal your main gift to you.

lifetimes, I believe we each have one main gift from God.

While many people may possess multiple spiritual gifts, I believe we miss an important opportunity to influence our lifetime priorities by not focusing upon one main gift, idea, or mission statement that God has gifted to us. Although most Bible studies challenge leaders to consider their multiple gifts, the Scriptures also challenge leaders to attend to a single gift or main purpose in life. "To each is given *the* manifestation of the Spirit for the common good" (1 Corinthians 12:7–8, italics added). "Serve one another with whatever *gift* each of you has received" (1 Peter 4:10, italics added). "For by the grace given to me I say to everyone among you not to think of yourself more highly than you ought to think, but to think with sober judgment, each according to *the* measure of faith that God has assigned" (Romans 12:3, italics added).

While these passages are often used to support the notion that each person possesses spiritual gifts from God, the passages actually use *gift* in the singular rather than plural. Rather than using these passages to suggest that each person has received at least one spiritual gift, I suggest that these passages challenge each of us to discover God's *main* purpose for our lives, a purpose that may be supported by multiple spiritual gifts. Discovering God's main purpose for our lives leads to the development of a personal vision. Spiritual gifts, on the other hand, become a part of the means of achieving that purpose. Discovering God's main gift involves discovering God's call or vocation for our lives. Discovering God's spiritual gifts provides part of the means of living out that call.

Not only do the Scriptures elicit exhortations to attend to our one main gift, the Bible provides real-life examples of individuals who were challenged to discover God's main purpose for their lives. As we have seen, Timothy was told not to neglect *the* gift that he had received. Later, he was challenged to rekindle *the* gift. The rich young ruler lacked *one* thing. Sheep hear *the* voice of the master. Jesus came to earth for *one* reason. Salt has *one* purpose. Although many leaders possess multiple gifts, at times all leaders must learn to be singularly focused. Henri Nouwen epitomized the benefits of being singularly focused and challenged his readers to do the same, "When man is not able to understand what is going on within himself … then words that come from above cannot penetrate into the center of his person. When emotions, ideas, and aspirations are cluttered together in an impermeable dirty crust, no dew can bring forth fruits and no clouds can 'rain on the just.'"[2] Utilizing our gifts can lead to success. Listening to the voice within that comes from God can take us beyond success. Faithful leaders hear the one true call of God.

The resource *A Guide to Prayer for Ministers and Other Servants,* contains twelve one-day retreat models for personal reflection, any of which may shed light upon your one main gift. More specifically, you may find models "One: God's Greatest Gift, Two: Called to Serve, and Eight: Sent Into the World" most helpful.[3]

Many more extensive tools exist that can help a person discover the main gift within. One of the best tools designed for establishing a single lifetime priority is *The Path* by Laurie Jones.[4] The book provides a variety of tools to aid the reader in mapping out a one-sentence personal lifetime mission statement. ChurchSmart Resources also offer a tool for personal mission statement discovery called *Focus.*[5] A personal mission statement is an invaluable product. Anyone willing to cultivate such a fruit will possess a substance with the potential to influence priorities throughout the rest of life.

In a similar manner to Laurie Jones, Rick Warren's book, *The Purpose Driven Church,* uses the acronym, SHAPE,[6] to challenge readers to focus upon the overall gift in a person's life.

S    stands for spiritual gifts.
H    stands for heart.
A    stands for abilities.
P    stands for personality.
E    stands for experiences.

Both Jones' and Warren's books approach the development of one's main gift inductively. Each book contains several exercises for the reader to follow. As each exercise is completed, the reader begins to build a big picture of God's purpose for his or her life. The exercises in Jones' book result in a mission statement. The exercises in Warren's book result in knowing one's unique ministry SHAPE. Whatever process is used, the development of one's main purpose in life can bring peace of mind and hope for the future. Attending to the main gift that God has given a person will bring about more satisfaction than any other potential task. In the end, that kind of focusing also will give life more meaning.

Do you want to be known for what you have done or who you have become? With no knowledge of your one main gift, you are destined to be known only for what you have done. Knowing your one main gift provides the pattern in the patchwork quilts of your life. It is the thread that weaves together your major experiences. It is not only useful for putting together the pattern of what has taken place, it is helpful in deciding which quilt block to add next. It informs your next step. Discerning your main gift can lead to a profitable understanding of your past and a prophetic navigation of your future.

### Peace of Mind

Discovering God's main purpose for my life provides a tremendous sense of satisfaction. On days when I am convinced that I am striving to accomplish God's will, I have a tremendous sense of satisfaction, even when those days are accompanied by complaints or crises. On days when I am ambiguous about God's will, I seldom have a sense of satisfaction, even when such days are accompanied by a worldly standard of success. Understanding God's main purpose for my life can bring a tremendous sense of peace both for the present moment and in future decision making.

Once a person has discovered God's main purpose for his or her life and developed a personal mission statement in order to articulate that purpose, such a statement can help that person choose among career choices, hobbies, support groups, vacations, friends, and even potential mates. It can help a person decide when to say, yes and when to say no. A personal mission statement helps a person discriminate appropriately among several options; it can affect every aspect of one's life, especially one's peace of mind.

My personal mission statement is, "to continually discover creative ways to accomplish God's mission." That is the thread that has run through each position I have held, each major contribution that I have offered, each task force on which I have served, each consulting assignment that I have accepted, etc.

If you have developed both a vision for your congregation and a personal mission statement at this stage of the process, then peace of mind could soon follow. Peace of mind is actually a byproduct of faithful leadership. Armed with a personal mission statement and a congregational vision, choosing from among potential opportunities becomes easier. Rather than weighing each opportunity against your current availability of time, you weigh it against your potential contribution to that task. "Is this opportunity consistent with my personal mission statement?" "Is this opportunity consistent with my congregation's vision?" A yes to both of these questions produces a yes to the opportunity. This simple process can even provide assistance in avoiding sleepless nights and stressful days. No matter what transpires from a single opportunity, one can always return to the two yeses to find comfort at night.

### Churches Model Their Pastors

While it is only informal and anecdotal in nature, I have been conducting my own little experiment in my role of constantly working with local congregations. When I visit a church that appears to be clearly focused on one part of its mission statement, I inquire about the senior pastor's style, approach, spiritual gifts, and personal mission statement. So far in my research, in every local church with a clearly observable short-term focus, whose pastor has been in leadership for more than three years, the focus is aligned with the pastor's personal mission statement. The easiest example to portray is a local church focused upon numerical growth. I have yet to interview the pastor of a numerically rapidly growing church who does not say that his or her *main* gift from God is evangelism! Additionally, churches that are solidly impacting their communities have pastors who have ministry at the core of their personal mission statement. Not just as one gift among the mix, but as the central gift. In some cases, this short-term emphasis also had been translated into a vision, but not in all cases. In other cases, the church recognizes that it exists for a variety of purposes, but one of those purposes consistently seems to receive more emphasis than the others.

Whether or not local congregations begin to take on the personality of the senior pastor is a question worth pursuing. In my brief history of questioning, this appears to be the case. I believe that discovering one's personal mission statement is an invaluable tool for a leader. Since it is at least a possibility that congregations may take on the personality of their leader, it also would be a good idea for search committees to ask potential candidates the personal-mission-statement question!

### Searching for That One Great Task

Consistently attending to one main gift can lead to accomplishing that one great task within a lifetime. Many famous individuals are known for one famous task. Many biblical characters are remembered for one great act of leadership, one great act of faithfulness. Most people would be satisfied with accomplishing one great task for God. The problem is that many of us spend so little time working our way toward a great task. Great tasks seldom fall into our laps. Attending to our main gift gets us to a great task. Sometimes we are assigned a great task by previously making excellent priority decisions in the past. Others work toward a great task by consistently choosing the higher ground. Getting to a great task is similar to negotiating a maze. If we consistently make the wrong choices, we will never get there.

The process a leader goes through to search for that one great task is similar to an actor pursuing that "one great script." If a leader consistently attends to things other than the one main gift, he or she may not even recognize that one great script when it arrives. Recognizing that script when the opportunity presents itself helps a leader accomplish that one great task. Actors consistently search for that one great script; continually choosing previous scripts wisely sends more and more potentially great scripts in their direction.

Recognizing a great script is not an easy task. It is both analytical and intuitive, requires both inward and outward guidance, and must be performed with both a keen focus and a great sense of peripheral vision. Choosing a great script can mean the difference between working on an award-winning script and working to make a script worthwhile. Most actors would rather receive an Academy Award rather than merely give an Academy Award–worthy performance. The difference is in the script. Many actors can rise above a script, but we seldom remember single performances apart from remembering the play itself. A great script gives a great actor a chance at a memorable play.

Although I must confess that its origin escapes me, one of my favorite sayings is, "Something not worth doing is not worth doing well." Give it a minute, the meaning will come. We have too many leaders with extraordinary skills working on very ordinary tasks in very ordinary places. I am convinced that mundane tasks are largely responsible for the outcry for stronger leaders. Faithful leaders look for the gem in every opportunity. The consistency of that faithfulness leads to great tasks and great accomplishments for God's kingdom.

We all know that church leaders do not actually deal with scripts; they deal with Scriptures. For faithful leaders, choosing the right task requires more than just insight. It requires God-sight. For faithful leaders, discernment is not only a part of the envisioning process: it is also a part of selection. Choosing the wrong task can result from a lack of prayer, reflection, Bible study, spiritual discussion, or accountability. Just as God must be the source of vision for a religious leader, God must also be the source of selection. God will help reveal the gifts to accomplish the vision. God's help must not be turned off after He has supplied the vision. Faithfulness must continue to build. Faithfulness must be present at every phase of discernment.

## Discovering Multiple Gifts

Once you have discovered how to attend to your main gift by establishing a personal mission statement or a clear purpose in life, another helpful exercise is to discover the full range of spiritual gifts God has given you that will help you live out your life's purpose. This task is probably more familiar to you than the one just emphasized. Discovering your spiritual gifts is an excellent way of preparing to accomplish the role God has given you. Many local churches offer excellent programs in spiritual-gift discovery. I believe that Charles Bryant has authored one of the most complete surveys available in the gift discovery process.[7]

In choosing a survey to discover your spiritual gifts, it is important to combine such a process with prayer, reflection, and discussion with a trusted friend. Test out your newly discovered insights with someone who can provide honest and loving feedback. Completion of a survey is merely the beginning of the insights that can be gained from understanding your spiritual gifts. Take the time to learn how others have used similar gifts. Learn how the gifts are spoken of in Scripture. What are the pitfalls for your particular gift? What are the potential joys? Take time to fully comprehend each gift that God has given you.

Throughout the discovery of your spiritual gifts, never lose sight of the single in the multiple. If you have developed a personal mission statement, integrate your spiritual gifts with your understanding of your personal mission statement. Continue to form the big picture. Integration is often a missing ingredient in many spiritual-gift discoveries.

I also would caution survey takers about identifying too many gifts at one time from such surveys. I am extremely skeptical about the magnitude of spiritual gifts that most programs produce for every individual taking the survey. Most surveys include a rating system. Upon completion of the survey, survey takers are asked to list their top three to five spiritual gifts. By design, every person taking the survey will end up with a list of spiritual gifts that includes three to five items. Although I regret that I am not aware of such a survey, I believe that a better way to reveal one's spiritual gifts would be to establish a threshold level necessary to qualify for a particular spiritual gift. Such a survey would probably require gathering data from many individuals but might prove to be worthwhile.

Although many congregations offer their members a variety of programs aimed at spiritual-gift discovery, fewer congregations offer useful suggestions in how to incorporate the news of such gifts into practical life applications. If your congregation takes the time to discover the spiritual gifts of members, challenge the leadership to use the information gleaned from such surveys. Challenge the nominating committee, the pastoral staff, the volunteer coordinator, and all the ministries of your church to look for those gifted for particular assignments, not just those willing to say yes to particular assignments! The *Network* is a resource that offers suggestions for integrating your spiritual gifts.[8] It is a program designed to take someone from gift discovery to gift utilization. It also contains helpful tools for integrating the knowledge of the gifts of members into the overall structure of the congregation.

# Rekindling

Rekindling a fire is much more difficult than keeping one going. Attending to your one main gift in life is easier than rekindling deadwood, driftwood, or wet wood. All three can require enormous amounts of energy. Although one process requires more work than the other, it also may carry greater rewards. As I work with volunteers and potential pastors who have finally decided to rekindle their leadership gift after neglecting it for several years, there is a sense of excitement and energy unequalled by those attending to their leadership gift for the first time.

# Wishing for More Gifts

I know … genies never allow you to make a wish wishing for more wishes. But God is not a genie. God is real and will find a way for you to reach your vision no matter how unlikely that may seem now. You may discover that even by attending to your personal gifts you still lack the gifts necessary to achieve the vision God has granted to your congregation. If this happens, ask God for more help! Trust God to supply your needs. Request the necessary gifts.

Do not limit your asking to God directly. Ask other servants of God. In a later chapter, I will present ideas related to drawing out the gifts of others that you may be leading through mentoring. For now, I simply challenge you to allow God to use creative ways of gifting you and those around you with the tools necessary to accomplish the vision. Some people prefer to think of the universal church as the body of Christ, while others suggest that a local congregation can be an expression of the body of Christ. Viewing your local congregation as one form of the body of Christ leads to an understanding and trust that God will use the variety of gifts within that body to achieve the common vision.

Some congregations have found it helpful to develop "wish lists" of other needed gifts. These lists can include, personnel (in the form of volunteers), land, capital improvements, and other items. The lists can be made available to small groups and individuals through newsletters, telephone calls, and personal visits. If God gave you the vision for your congregation, then there must be a way of achieving it. Trust God to supply the means as well as the ends, but do not be afraid to ask.

---

1   *Leonard Sweet,* A Cup of Coffee at the Soul Café *(Nashville: Broadman & Holman Publishers, 1998), 60.*

2   *Henri J. Nouwen,* Creative Ministry *(Garden City, N.Y.: Image Books, 1971), 36.*

3   *Reuben P. Job, and Norman Shawchuck,* A Guide to Prayer for Ministers and Other Servants *(Nashville: The Upper Room, 1983).*

4   *Laurie Beth Jones,* The Path: Crating Your Mission Statement for Work and for Life *(New York: Hyperion, 1996).*

5   *Focus may be ordered from ChurchSmart Resources, 350 Randy Road #5, Carol Stream, IL 60188, (800) 253–4276.*

6   *Rick Warren,* The Purpose Driven Church *(Grand Rapids, Mich.: Zondervan Publishing Company, 1972), 370.*

7   *Charles Bryant,* Rediscovering our Spiritual Gifts: Building Up the Body of Christ through the Gifts of the Spirit *(Nashville: The Upper Room, 1991).*

8   *Bruce Bugbee, Don Cousins, and Bill Hybels,* Network: Understanding God's Design for You in the Church *(Grand Rapids, Mich.: Zondervan Publishing House, 1994).*

# 3

## PRIORITIZING TO PLEASE GOD

**A**LL LEADERS SEEK TO PLEASE SOMEONE. SOME try to please the customer. Other leaders try to please a board of directors. Still others try to please a boss, a bottom line, or a band of employees. Faithful leaders strive to please God. They do so by regularly setting priorities that advance God's vision. This chapter will encourage faithful leaders to focus their daily efforts upon pleasing God by setting priorities that advance the vision discovered from God. Since "prioritizing" is the most fundamental task of leadership, it also is the most consistent means for a leader to please God.

Every role has its most fundamental task. For the leadership role, the most fundamental task is prioritizing. It is not the most important, but it is the most fundamental. It is at the base and core of leadership. Choosing between options is the most common type of decision that a leader makes. What will you emphasize during the coming year? How will you decide what to place on the next agenda? What will you do on Monday? What will you do first each day? What will you discard from last year? Which new thing will you do this year? Leadership is about setting priorities. Novice leaders become veteran leaders by consistently choosing the right priorities and by consistently learning from poor priority decisions. People in charge of little are placed in charge of much by choosing the right priorities and by being faithful.

The leadership process unravels like this ... God supplies the vision. Then the members of the congregation affirm that vision. The leaders discover and attend to the gifts within themselves that can contribute toward that vision. Finally, the leaders carry out the vision on a daily basis by setting priorities. If leaders would consistently strive to please God in the priorities that they set, many of the other tasks of leadership would also naturally fall into the status of being faithful to God.

# Setting Personal Priorities

Whether we realize it or not, we do have control over our own agendas. Others may make demands upon us as leaders, but we choose which demands to act upon. When faced with a decision or an opportunity, it is important to respond to that opportunity in a manner that will maximize the contribution of the leader to that task.

When I asked the newly elected chairperson of our local Habitat for Humanity chapter (also a member of the congregation that I was pastoring) what I could do to help, she responded, "Give me one hour a week to help me see the big picture of where we are headed." That one hour allowed me to maximize my contribution to that organization. I was able to use my main gift, helping groups find creative ways of accomplishing God's mission, in a way that benefited a member of my church and potentially would bring benefit to a community ministry. When we make decisions that maximize our main gifts, we discover that such tasks energize us rather than drain us. This is the secret to accomplishing a great deal in a limited amount of time. If most of the tasks that we do leave us exhausted, too much time will be spent replenishing our tank in order to tackle the next assignment. Faithful leaders set priorities that allow them to joyfully advance the God-given vision and mission for their organization.

### Developing a Personal Goals List

Setting priorities that consistently utilize our main gifts and advance God's vision will not happen by accident. We must have plans. As leaders make plans, they begin with the broad and work toward the narrow. That is precisely the way that this book has been organized. The most important aspect of leadership is for each of us to discover God's vision for our group. Then, we must discover the main gifts that God has given us that might contribute toward that vision. Finally, we come to the point of actually making decisions that influence that vision. But, even as we make plans, we begin with the broad and work toward the narrow. Faithful leaders plan for the coming year before they plan what to do on Monday. That is because the plans for the coming year will affect the plans for Monday.

One way of prioritizing the coming year is to develop a personal goals list each year. It is a personal management task I would recommend for every faithful leader. What transforms this management task into a leadership task is prioritizing. The most important part of this task is reflection. Near the end of your leadership year, spend a significant amount of time analyzing your goals and accomplishments from that year. Never limit your analysis to your official goals list from the previous year. Also reflect upon those events that arose during the course of the year that cried out for leadership but could not be foreseen ahead of time.

As you analyze your accomplishments, begin to make a list of the things you would like to accomplish next year. Do not automatically add items to next year's list that were not accomplished during the past year. There may be a very good reason why particular items were not given much energy or priority. Be careful about repeating events two years in a row, unless you want them to become annual events. Most people find that it helps to categorize similar types of goals. My annual goals list will normally include items in the following categories: administration, programming, enhancing organizational relationships, representation, and personal. Other categories are added or deleted in order to relate more specifically to the current vision or annual theme. Review your list asking such questions as, "Will these priorities please God?" "Will these priorities advance God's vision for this organization?" "Are these priorities worthy of a God as merciful and powerful as ours?"

The last step in forming your personal goals list for the coming year is to mark every item with an E or a D. For every type of item that normally energizes you (leaves you with more energy than when you began the task), mark it with an E. Conversely, for every item that normally drains you (leaves you with less energy at the end than at the beginning), mark it with a D. This step may cause you to make some adjustments to your list, especially if you have more D's than E's. It also may prompt a trip to the career center!

### Developing a Personal Goals List
1. Reflect upon last year's accomplishments.
2. Review both goals and unexpected opportunities.
3. Compile a list of goals for next year.
4. Categorize the list.
5. Mark every item with a "D" (draining activity) or an "E" (energizing activity).

## Perpetual Calendars

Once you have established your personal goals list for the coming year, I strongly encourage you to add at least one more step to the process. If you are not a strong J according to the Myers-Briggs Personality Inventory, you may not have made it this far in this personal organization section. But, for the J's who are still reading, let's plow ahead!

In addition to an annual goals list, I maintain a kind of personal perpetual calendar. While the personal goals list helps you plan *what* to do during the coming year, the perpetual calendar helps you plan *when* to do it. A perpetual calendar can prevent you from playing catch-up during the year around major annual events. In order to establish the perpetual calendar for the first time, simply keep track of the major items that you do during the year. Include such items as preparing for a presentation, publicizing an event, sending out meeting notices, etc. You will find that you need to prepare for certain events in similar ways at similar times of the year. Once you have established a personal perpetual calendar, spend some time each year removing unnecessary items that will not need to be repeated next year due to a change in vision, theme, or emphasis as well as moving items around in order to be better prepared next year. You will probably end up with a calendar that contains several items for each month of the coming year. Think of each month's items as the start of your to-do list for that particular month. One of the benefits of possessing a perpetual calendar is the ability to build in your own heavy and slow periods according to vacations, favorite seasons, etc.

In order to position yourself to make priority decisions that will please God by advancing his vision, integrate your annual goals list with your perpetual calendar. Your annual goals list should contain a list of those tasks that will be new to the coming year in order to advance the particular theme established or the particular phase of God's short-term vision that you happen to be in. Your perpetual goals list should contain a list of those tasks that must be done every year in order to carry on God's long-term mission for your organization. Place each item contained on your annual goals list into one of the months on your perpetual calendar for the coming year. You will be adding to your to-do list for each month. Be sure to maintain your desired peak and slow times and be sure to spread out the D and E items. When I transfer my annual goals list to my monthly perpetual calendar, I make sure that I build in one creative project to work on during each quarter. I need that to energize me. A different type of task may energize you. Whatever it may be, evenly spread your most energizing projects throughout the year.

*Developing a Personal Perpetual Calendar*
1. Keep a diary of your major activities for one year.
2. Include all major events.
3. Divide the list into months.
4. Review last year's calendar.
5. Delete or delegate certain items.
6. Rearrange as necessary.
7. Add items from your current personal goals list.

## To-Do Lists

If you currently use a to-do list that is shorter than a month in length, such as a weekly or daily one, I have one last suggestion. On a monthly basis, transfer activities from the monthly perpetual calendar to your weekly or daily to-do list. As I record this process, I realize that it sounds like a lot of work, but it will reap great benefits. This type of planning guarantees that you will focus upon activities that both energize you as a leader and advance God's vision for your congregation. I spend about two weeks out of every year, usually one in December and one in January, reflecting, removing, adding, and most important ... prioritizing my annual list of goals and my perpetual calendar. It is usually during "driving time" that I prioritize my weekly to-do list. Transferring my monthly priorities to my weekly to-do lists simply ensures that I will accomplish what I told my personnel committee I would accomplish during the coming year.

The detailed process list above may be scaled up or down depending upon your specific leadership situation. I do not mean to imply that the process must be lengthy in order to be worthwhile. Some may be leading groups of congregations or serving as CEOs of large nonprofit organizations. Others may be leading small groups of three people. Size is irrelevant. Prioritizing, however, is relevant. It is the key to effective leadership. Prioritizing in ways that please God leads us to become faithful leaders. Priorities that advance God's vision and mission for the congregation are those that become pleasing to God.

Faithful leaders are not merely leaders who pray a lot. Faithful leaders are not merely leaders who focus upon spiritual matters. Faithful leaders are those who strive to please God every day through the priorities they establish. Leonard Sweet writes, "The closer Jesus came to God's presence, the more strongly the God within became evident to those around him."[1]

No matter how long or short your list of prime activities that will advance the vision, it is not necessary for the leader to perform every task. Rather, the leader must constantly question whether or not he or she should be doing the task at hand. Are you the best person to do that task? If not, assign or recruit someone else to do it. As suggested in the previous chapter, consistently strive to attend to your main gift as you perform as a leader.

### Paying the Dues

Setting priorities that will advance the current vision of your congregation and keep you energized as a leader does not mean that you can ignore the mission statement of your congregation. Remember that a vision is a narrowly defined picture of where God wants your congregation to be in the near future. Working to advance God's vision actually carries us beyond success toward faithfulness. Accomplishing this vision, however, cannot be done at the expense of neglecting the basic mission of your congregation. We all must "pay the dues of belonging."

When I worked as a local church pastor, I had a system of setting weekly priorities that allowed me to accomplish a major task every week and still take a day off! On Sunday evening, I prioritized my weekly to-do list, putting those events first that would most likely advance God's vision and most likely yield the highest results according to the 80–20 Pareto Principle.[2] Through reflection and prioritization, I often discovered that the week's most pressing project was not always the week's most important project. Weekly worship services and weekend conversations always influenced weekly priority lists. Do not fret if you are not accustomed to working with written to-do lists. Even those who despise to-do lists can intuitively discern the week's most important projects. On Monday morning I finished my sermons for the coming Sunday. (By the time Monday morning came, a rough draft of the sermons would usually already be in place or at least a folder of notes from which to draw.) On Monday afternoon I contacted all of the people whom Sunday parishioners had told me that I should contact the day before. On Tuesday morning I worked on the most important task for the week other than the sermons. My Tuesday morning project was always chosen according to the priorities established in my weekly to-do list. I chose my Tuesday-morning project on the basis of which project would most advance God's vision. On Monday, I finished my preparations for Sunday. On Tuesday, I accomplished the next most salient task of the week.

Every Monday and Tuesday I paid the dues. On Wednesday, I sought personal renewal … every week. (Our midweek service was on Thursday evening.) With my sermons ready and my most important task completed, most weeks I truly enjoyed my day off. On Thursday and Friday I tried to work ahead on other projects, meet with people about programming issues, conduct research for future sermons, etc. If Monday and Tuesday can be characterized by paying the dues, Thursday and Friday could be characterized by working on the passions. For me, the most rewarding part of a task is at the beginning when all of the options are still open. I paid the dues on Monday and Tuesday in order to get to the more creative parts of the projects on Thursday and Friday. Others may find more satisfaction in arranging a different set of tasks for the Monday/Tuesday and Thursday/Friday combination. Adapt the model as needed. For me, the model worked well. Pay the dues on Monday and Tuesday. Enjoy Wednesday. Work on the passions Thursday and Friday.

Just in case anyone is wondering, the answer is, "Yes! There were many weeks when this perfect little schedule was interrupted, even obliterated." But if a crisis or a funeral occurred in the latter part of the week, putting everything planned for Thursday and Friday on hold, I knew that I already had accomplished the most important aspects for the week. If the crisis occurred at the beginning of the week, my Monday/Tuesday routine was performed on Thursday/Friday.

I'll admit that I have not been as regular with my day off in my new role. I have discovered that the tasks in my current position require a longer cycle than before. There are busier seasons and there are actually more "down times" than in the pastorate. I now try to take a couple of days off during slower seasons rather than one day off a week. Believe it or not, the slower seasons now occur around holidays. My current role involves working with local congregations. Local congregations are usually busy doing their own thing during the holidays. Conflicts even diminish. My current work rhythm is probably similar to the members of the church rather than the pastoral leadership.

## Setting Priorities for Your Congregation

In order to advance God's vision for your congregation, prioritizing not only your own activities, but also the activities of the congregation you are leading is important. Prioritizing is the most common task of leadership. How can you prioritize the tasks for the group you are leading in a way that will please God? Remember, it is prioritizing that transforms a management task into a leadership task, and it is prioritizing to please God that transforms the process into a faithful one. Constantly ask, "What is God's vision for our congregation?" and then follow through by prioritizing accordingly.

### Designing Annual Themes

One way to establish priorities within your congregation is to emphasize a particular goal during the coming year. The source of the goal can be obtained by breaking down your vision into manageable pieces each year or highlighting different aspects of God's vision. It has been said that an organization can only truly hope to alter the behavior of its members in one area each year. Rather than being tossed about by periodic waves and opportunities, think ahead to what you want that one main thing to be!

The short-term vision for the organization in which I minister is to perform every task as a ministry task. Our motto is "Make Ministry Job #1." Thus, every year, our annual themes emphasize some aspect of ministry. Our last four annual themes have been:

- *A Call to Prayer.* During this year, our nearly 300 congregations were divided into six subgroups. The subgroups of fifty prayed for one of their congregations on a weekly basis according to specific requests from that congregation. That same week, the congregation being prayed for was given materials encouraging them to focus on prayer.

- *Winning Ohio for Christ.* Our denominational theme for ministries with a national scope is, "America for Christ." This theme focused on evangelism through a connection with the wider denomination.

- *Rooted in the Word, Alive in the World.* Staff developed three questions a day to coincide with a one-chapter-a-day Bible-reading emphasis for members of all congregations. We also distributed testimonies of people in the workplace.

- *Ministry for the Millenium: Impacting Individuals, Communities and the World (Acts 1:8).* During this emphasis, every member of every congregation was encouraged to name a ministry. Every congregation was encouraged to "adopt" something ... an adjacent block, a nursing home, a school, a senior center, the newlyweds in their community, etc., and encouraged to develop a partnership with a mission agency beyond their local community.

As you can see, the themes become more involved each year as we strive to advance God's vision.

Many local congregations also find the use of annual themes helpful. Some sample themes include:

- Benevolent people
- Celebrating Christ
- Everyone a minister
- Sola Scriptura
- Building on our heritage
- Faith for the future

### Prioritizing the Coming Year

An annual theme provides a broad focus for the coming year. Details must still be added to advance the vision and emphasize the theme. You may be tempted to view the development of a congregational vision and theme as a leadership process and the remaining tasks as management. Establishing the congregational calendar for the coming year can either be a management task or a leadership task. If the major task is planning, then it is a management task. If the major task is prioritizing, then it becomes a leadership task. I have described below a prioritizing process that I use near the end of every organizational year in order to establish a calendar for the following year that will continue to advance God's vision and, ultimately, please God.

Toward the end of the year, list five events or decisions that you think people will remember about the preceding year of your organization in the coming years. You can do this either personally or with a group. As you list the events, look for patterns that will help you decide what to plan for or emphasize next year. To aid your process, use the following questions:

- Ten years from now, what events will people remember about this year's work?
- What do these events have in common?
- What are the emerging trends?
- Were the events planned?
- Were any of the events a response to outside circumstances?
- Did anyone else get involved that made it memorable?
- Was it well attended? Why?

- Who emphasized the event?
- To what extent was the memorable nature of the event due to quality leadership?
- How did the event help us fulfill God's vision for our congregation?
- How could quality leadership re-create or enhance similar events in future years?

Often what was planned to be memorable does not end up being remembered as a key event in future years. Almost always, other spontaneous events or even simple ordinary events become memorable due to unforeseen circumstances surrounding the event. What events might fall into the memorable category for the coming year? Choose three to five events that potentially have a memorable quality to them. Your list may include some events that your group is responsible for on an annual basis. If this is so, try to plan the event in such a way that it will become memorable year after year. Try to include at least one brand-new event every year.

If you do not want an event to become an annual tradition, do not repeat it two years in a row. Doing so will force the leadership to explain why the event is being "dropped" in some future year. It is much easier to bring back an event periodically rather than to explain why you chose not to repeat it after years of tradition. And in most churches, two years makes a tradition! Sometimes even powerful events should not be repeated on an annual basis. The reason? There are only so many volunteers and resources to go around each year. That is the "widgets" lecture in economics 101. Some organizations spend so much time planning, designing, promoting, and producing one or two annual events, that little, if any energy, is left to do anything new during the coming year. Think twice about repeating even a memorable event the very next year. Always ask the question, "What else could we do if we were not doing this?" That is the "opportunity costs" lecture in economics 101.

Allow the list of three to five potentially memorable events to form the bedrock of your prioritization calendar for the coming year. Be sure to follow through in your leadership and give these events top priority during the coming year. Spacing the events somewhat evenly throughout the year will allow you to emphasize each one when it comes along. Prioritizing an annual calendar for your congregation is the best way to keep you and your congregation vibrant year after year. It also is an excellent way to please God.

### Prioritizing Committee Meetings

Eventually, leaders will be called upon to lead meetings. At this point, don't allow all of the previous prioritizing to go to waste. If you developed a perpetual calendar or a list of personal goals or a list of potentially memorable events, emphasize those priorities at your committee meetings. One way to do this is to begin the meeting with a devotional thought that reflects your current emphasis. Another way is to recite or recall your priorities at each meeting. If God has placed a vision in front of you as a leader and you have found a way to make the vision plain for the people you are leading, it will not be difficult to lift up the vision at each meeting. If, however, you have to look up the vision to remember what it says, the chances of emphasizing that vision at committee meetings will greatly decrease.

One way of prioritizing committee meetings is to establish a categorical agenda. A categorical agenda involves "forcing" every agenda item into a set of preestablished classifications. Choose classifications that match the current vision of your organization. If your current emphasis relates to ministry, include a category for "ministry updates" not just "news" and look for "ministry opportunities" not just "future happenings." You might choose to include your current theme or emphasis as one of the agenda items at every meeting in order to ensure that some discussion takes place relative to your theme.

As an alternative, you may choose a set of classifications that matches your personal leadership style. One that I have used in the past is:

- Envision
- Evaluate
- Change
- Look for opportunities

The most important thing to remember is that, as the person leading the meeting, you have the greatest opportunity for leadership prior to the start of the meeting. Choosing how to start a meeting, choosing what to place on the agenda, choosing how to order the items, and choosing how to allocate discussion time to the items are all priority decisions. Thus, they are leadership decisions. Do not neglect the prime leadership role that you are given by simply "going with the flow" at committee meetings or ignoring the valuable role of meeting preparation.

Faithful leaders prioritize by looking for the gem in each day, each agenda, each calendar, and each lifetime. What tasks within your organization lie dormant, awaiting only your sense of urgency and excitement as you move those tasks up the priority scale? Prioritize your activities in such a manner that God's vision for your congregation will become evident to others and most important of all, pleasing to God.

---

1  *Sweet,* A Cup of Coffee, 54.

2  *The Pareto Principle refers to an 80\20 ratio that exists in many situations. For instance, 20 percent of the people in an organization often accomplish 80 percent of its mission. For information on the Pareto Principle, consult C. Jeff Woods,* We've Never Done It Like This Before, *Bethesda, Md.: Alban Institute, 1994.*

# 4

## REDEEMING CRISES

IN PREVIOUS CHAPTERS, WE LOOKED AT THE IMPORtance of discovering God's vision for your congregation. We also noted the importance of discovering your main gift as a leader in order to assess your contribution to that vision. In the last chapter, the saliency of setting daily priorities that will advance the vision was the focus. The heart of this chapter challenges you as a faithful leader not to ignore the vision, the gifts, and the priorities of your organization even in the midst of a crisis.

Ephesians 5:16 contains one of the most peculiar phrases to translate in the New Testament. The New Revised Standard Version translates it, "making the most of the time." The Contemporary English Version translates the phrase, "so make every minute count." The Jerusalem Bible translates the verse, "(This may be a wicked age), but your lives should redeem it." The New English Bible translates it, "Use the present opportunity to the full."

Numerous translations for a particular passage usually arise from peculiar configurations of words among the manuscripts. Such is the case here. The manuscripts for this phrase contain only two words. The first word means "to redeem." The second word is *kairos*. There is no English word that adequately conveys the meaning of *kairos*.

When faced with previous dilemmas of this nature, many English-speaking people have created a new English word from a transliteration of the Greek word. To illustrate, many congregations have introduced the word *agape* into their vocabulary in order to better portray the love of God, the word *koinonia* to better portray God's sense of community, and the word *shalom* to better portray God's idea of peace.

I believe that the word *kairos* is another word that needs to become a part of the vocabulary of English speaking congregations. It is a word that means, "full of meaning," literally, "pregnant with meaning." Words such as "opportunity" or "prospect" do not adequately portray the meaning of kairos. Certain moments in life are full of meaning, alive with potential. Unfortunately, we often view such moments as potential crises rather than potential victories. That is because such moments are also laden with change and we historically avoid moments that are full of change rather than embrace such moments. Faithful leaders, however, are called to redeem such moments for God. Rather than being devastated by potential predicaments, we are called to turn crisis moments into kairos moments. God challenges us to see the opportunity amidst every emergency.

Finding a crisis in order to redeem a kairos moment should not be difficult. We often do not have to look very far. There appears to be no shortage of available crises for church leaders today! Facing crises has become a regular item on the job descriptions of church leaders. As recently as one generation ago, many local church programs and emphases were clicking like clockwork. Nearly every local church in America was growing numerically, and numerical growth (although unhealthy to promote by itself), staved off many potential crises. Today, the landscape has changed. Due to the rapid changes within church and society, it is much more difficult today to be a church leader than it was just one generation ago. Appropriately, some are asking, "Where have all the green dots gone?"

# No More Green Dots

A few years ago I had the opportunity to speak at a series of meetings in Banff, Canada, held by the Baptist Union of Western Canada. I delivered my messages during the evening hours and had my afternoons free. During the first afternoon, I was asked what I would like to do during my free time. At my request, I was given a set of maps and took advantage of the beautiful scenery in the Canadian Rockies. The mountains were breathtaking. During the second afternoon, I was given a different set of maps leading to destinations where I might encounter natural wildlife. They were right. I had not been traveling more than fifteen minutes when I saw a sign for a bighorn sheep crossing. Right next to the sign, as if on cue, was a bighorn sheep! The scenery once again captivated me, and the Canadians were struck by my enthusiasm. On the third afternoon, my host suggested, "If you really want a view of these mountains, you ought to go skiing. Do you snow ski?" came the question rather innocently.

"Yes, I snow ski," I replied, adding softly, "on the mountains of Indiana."

Desiring to increase my enthusiasm, my host suggested, "You'll love the view from these mountains," and he handed me my third set of maps.

Seeing the view of the mountains as a part of the landscape rather than from afar truly intrigued me. Navigating the landscape, however, intimidated me. As I rented my skis, I was full of questions. "Just how big are these mountains?" "How long does it take to get down?" "What if I fall?" "Are the trails marked?"

"Yes, sir. Every trail is clearly marked. Green dots indicate the easy runs. Blue squares highlight intermediate runs, and black diamonds … Well, just stay away from the black diamonds."

In an effort to verify this newly received information, I asked the person at the gondola, "So, the green dots are the easy runs, huh?"

"Sir. You've skied before, eh?"

"Yes," I replied with limited confidence.

"Well, you won't be on the green dots very long. Don't bother getting off at the first stop," he said as he bolted the gondola door shut and waved good-bye.

"How does he know I won't be on the green dots very long? I planned on camping out there for the duration! Wait a minute. The first stop is not as far up the mountain." I began my usual set of musings, which usually led to trouble. Thinking too much can be a very bad habit. But bad habits are also difficult to break. "I need all of the green dots I can get," I continued in a conversation directed to my rational side. "I don't care what he said, I'm getting off at the first stop. I don't care if I'm the only adult on the bunny hills today. That won't embarrass me."

As I arrived at the first stop, I continued my musings. "Hmmm. No children around. No adults, either for that matter. Maybe everyone in Canada is so experienced that no one stops at these bunny trails anymore. It's late in the skiing season. Plenty of time to graduate from the bunny trails. There's a chairlift. It doesn't look too bad. I can't really see past that fog, but I'll... . "

As I passed through what I had determined to be fog, but later discovered had been a cloud, the vista opened up and I was once again captivated by the majesty of the mountains. So captivated, I didn't realize how long it was taking to get to the top. But, all the while, I was naively appreciating my surroundings. "It's so nice of the people to put the green dots here. I can't imagine a more beautiful spot on these slopes. I will just stay here in the green-dot section all day and not even attempt anything tougher." I arrived at the top. The "virtual" disappeared from my reality. First run ... black diamond. Second run ... double black diamond. Third run ... another black diamond. I scurried to every possible exit discovering only black diamonds.

"I've got to get off this mountain! What did I do to myself! My wife told me not to do anything crazy, and here I am on the top of this black-diamond mountain. She'll never even visit me in the hospital if she knows how I got into this mess!"

"I know. I'll just ride the ski lift back down!" Those who have tried this know it doesn't work. The lift slows down to let off passengers, but quickly speeds up once again as it continues around the corner. The speed prevents one from descending in the same manner as the ascent. I would have asked someone for help, but no one else was coming up this mountain. (Duh.) Finally, a fellow skier ascended the mountain.

"I sure am glad to see you," I said. "What's the easiest way down?"

"You've skied before, eh?"

"Yes," I said, tiring of such inquiries.

"Well, try that run over there," he pointed without ever coming to a complete stop and quickly disappearing over the edge.

I moved quickly toward the spot where he had pointed. "It doesn't look too bad. Maybe I can do this." I started down. "Hey, this is not too bad. Remember. Side to side. Whoa!" The trail dropped straight down as I turned the next corner. I was terrified. "Hey, no one said I had to ski down this mountain. I'll just sit down!" Sitting was much less intimidating, but also much more difficult to stay on the trail. My suspicions of being off the trail were indeed confirmed when I encountered a sign, "Avalanche Area." I picked up my skis, headed back to the trail, recited the Twenty-third Psalm, and only by the grace of God made it down the mountain in one piece.

Once back at the conference, my host, Gerry Fisher, inquired, "Did you go skiing today."

"Yes," I said.

"Hey, did you make it up Goat's Eye?" he said, chuckling in anticipation of a response similar to, "No way!"

"As a matter of fact, I did," I replied, not yet recognizing the magnitude of that mountain.

"Oh, quite the skier, eh?" he said.

"Not exactly," I replied as I quickly revealed how my experience consisted more of fear than of confidence. Gerry proceeded to inform me of just how intimidating that mountain could be even to the locals. Its intimidation will never subside for me. I will never be a "local," and

I will never again try to navigate the black diamonds of Goat's Eye.

For many church leaders today, black diamonds are not optional. Amidst a landslide of change, many of today's church leaders are asking, "Where have all the green dots gone? Nothing seems to be easy anymore." Just one generation ago, American church leaders were in the glory days. Every single attempted program succeeded. We announced it, and they followed. We built it, and they came. We preached it, and they were changed. Not so anymore. Many church leaders must attempt a variety of approaches before they settle on one that intrigues their neighborhood or their current membership. Reaching every new group requires a different set of approaches.

The first reaction of many bitten by the nostalgia of previous church success is to long for the "good ol' days." "Oh, if we could just go back twenty or thirty years ago to the way things used to be." Such reminiscers quickly discover that there is no way to get back on the chairlift.

Our second reaction often is to take the changes sitting down rather than standing up. "I'll change, but I won't change at the pace of society. That is just too fast for me! I'll take this sitting down." Such decisions usually unveil even more hazardous outcomes ... avalanches, conflicts, budget enigmas, and leadership puzzlements.

Perhaps we simply need to come to terms with the fact that all the green dots are gone for today's church leaders. There are no more programs that will work in every situation. There are no more easy answers. It is no longer appropriate for a denomination to sell one quick-fix program as a solution to multiple situations. The old methods consisted of passing along the newest denominational resource. The new methods consist of trial and error, prayer and reflection, wrestling and change. Change is the name of the game these days, and I fear that we are only in the early stages of this game.

There is no short supply of crises in today's world. It seems that a new event laden with opportunity lies around every corner. Opportunistic catastrophes in church life surface much more regularly today than in previous generations. Many believe that the abundance of change in today's society and today's organizations is one of the prime reasons for the disappearance of the green dots.

## An Abundance of Change

Change is not new. Every day since creation the world has changed. Over time, rivers change direction; glaciers form and melt; forests totally replenish their trees and wildlife. Today's changes, however, are more dramatic, more visible, and more closely tied to leadership than ever before. Today's external changes impact leaders of congregations in a greater way than previous generations for two reasons.

First, changes occur more quickly than they used to. The rate or speed of change is greater today than even one generation ago. Old methods of retrieving information are not sufficient to stay on the cutting edge of today's informational stream. "It is a white-water world," suggests Stephen Covey. "In all sectors—business, government, health care, social, or non-profit—the marketplace is demanding that organizations transform themselves."[1]

This increase in the rate of change has affected church leaders more than any other discipline or profession. Like all leaders, church leaders are expected to stay current in fields that directly affect their work, such as biblical studies, theology, and worship. Many churches also expect their leaders, however, to stay current on a host of other fields as well, such as counseling, administration, and computers. Church leaders are expected to be both experts in spiritual matters and generalists in many others. Most church leaders have long discovered that it is impossible to stay current in multiple fields, let alone maintaining a cutting edge ability in several fields. Until such realizations are negotiated with the members of the congregation, the current rate of change will continue to create headaches for church leaders.

When the body of leadership within a congregation has not kept pace with new information, a crisis can ensue. Lack of awareness of employee practices can result in lawsuits. Lack of counseling safeguards can lead to victimization. Faithful leaders have abandoned the old ideas of church leadership success that assume the pastor is the expert in every field. Instead, they view the crises that arise from the lack of expertise as kairos moments to involve others in the life of the congregation.

I still remember sitting in on a conversation between my potential web-page host and my newly recruited web master. I understood less than 10 percent of that conversation, and that is probably being personally generous! Never be embarrassed by calling for help. No one expects the leader to know everything. People do, however, expect leaders to stay abreast of the areas that most affect their ability to perform their tasks.

The second reason that today's changes are adversely affecting leaders is that the places where changes most often occur are places that affect organizations and their leaders. Technology is the hotbed for today's changes; technology most commonly affects information and communication, the tools of leaders. Just as a pipe fitter would be devastated if someone suddenly replaced all of his old tools with new ones, so are today's leaders devastated by rapid changes in information and communication technology. Such changes within today's world, "force people to learn whole new ways of ... communicating with one another."[2] When change affects an organization, the members of the organization naturally look to the organizational leader to be both map reader and scout. It is not just the fact that there are rapid changes in our world; the changes themselves are of the type that strike at the heart of organizations and their leaders.

## Creating Kairos by Redeeming Crises

Now that we are convinced that there is no shortage of external crises in today's world, the how-to question must be posed, "How do you redeem such moments?" A faithful leader creates kairos moments by advancing the mission and vision of the congregation in the midst of a crisis. This is not a natural task for leaders. When the person at the other end of the phone, or the other side of your desk, or the other edge of your office rug is discombobulated, disappointed, or infuriated, the natural tendency is to forget about your organization altogether and solve *that* person's problem. But, a leader does not cease being the leader of his or her organization in the midst of a crisis.

When emotions are high, often, so is the potential for redemption. Consider how many times Jesus turned heated moments into kairos moments ... when the people had gathered with stones in their hands ... when the crowd had gone three days without food ... when the people were shouting "hosannas" ... when Peter held the ear in his hand. I am convinced that Jesus had God's mission in mind each time that he responded to a potential calamity. Likewise, Jesus calls us to bring kairos out of the jaws of crisis, rather than merely to diffuse or dissolve the situation. We create kairos moments by seeking to advance God's mission in the midst of the crisis. That's what faithful leaders do. Even when changes and crises come fast and furiously, faithful leaders are called to advance God's mission. We do that by saying to the people who are following us, "We can respond to this crisis in many ways, but if we respond in this manner, I believe that we will be doing what God has called our congregation to do. I believe that we can actually advance God's vision if we take this course."

### Creating a Climate of Expected Change

Responding to a crisis is always easier if people believe that change is commonplace in your organization. Often, the threat of change itself can be more intimidating than the outcomes posed by the change. For an organization familiar with change, this is not the case. Advancing God's vision amidst a sea of change involves consistently reminding members that responding to the changes will create something better for your organization. Judith Bardwick writes, "Today and far into the future, leaders must convince people that dealing with unending change not only is necessary but also will result in something better."[3]

Sometimes leaders misinterpret statements of anxiety as attempts to block the current vision or emphasis. One example of this is when a person uses the phrase, "Well, we've certainly never done it like that before." Leaders sometimes misinterpret such phrases too quickly as "killer phrases," when in reality such phrases simply may be a manner of releasing anxiety. Rather than combatting such statements, build upon them. Use such verbal releases to create a climate of change within your congregation. In a previous congregation that I pastored, the phrase, "We've never done it like this before" actually became a mantra for change rather than a statement of defeatism. Whenever someone would feel nervous about a change that was occurring, the person would chuckle and say, "Well, we've never done it like this before." Others around would nod their heads in agreement and then bond together to tackle the change.

Another way to create a climate of change is to add a category entitled "Change" to every agenda within your committee or staff meeting. Calling attention to such fluidity within your congregation will create a climate of change and make it easier for your congregation to respond to changes within your own context and the contexts of your constituents. "A higher rate of urgency does not imply ever present panic, anxiety, or fear. It means a state in which complacency is virtually absent, in which people are always looking for both problems and opportunities, and in which the norm is, 'do it now.'"[4]

### Floods, Earthquakes, and Pestilences

Not all of today's crises occur as a result of the rapid changes in today's world. Natural disasters are another form of crisis that call for immediate response from God's people. God's faithful leaders also will find a way to advance God's vision in the midst of natural disasters.

Soon after I came to my present position of working with the American Baptist Churches in Ohio, the Ohio River flooded in the

Cincinnati Area. I had just announced a motto of "Making Ministry Job #1." Such a crisis would have called for a response regardless of our motto, but the motto suggested an avenue of responding to the crisis. We sought to advance the ministries of our local church partnerships by mobilizing the member churches to respond.

One particular Saturday, I was teamed with a small group of volunteers from the Urbana area. I will admit that I was unprepared for what I found as we removed all of the possessions from the home of a tenant along the river. The smell, the filth, and the dead creatures quickly explained the need for the tetanus shot that I had received moments before. My expectations of helping these people "get a little water out of their basements" were shattered. Nothing could be salvaged. Possibly due to the smell and possibly due to our anxiety, our group worked quickly. So quickly, that the landlord instructed us also to remove the contents of the other half of the duplex in which we had been working. Near the end of that task, the owner of the items arrived back at the residence. We quickly discovered that she, personally, had not given permission for her items to be removed. Although removal of the contents was inevitable at some point, the breakdown in communication nearly led to a breakdown of our bones and vehicles. Once we saw that our attempts at reasoning and our offers to return the items were vehemently rejected, we left the scene.

One of the pastors in our group reported this instance to his congregation the next morning, upon which, the congregation had this reaction, "Apparently, this woman did not understand the reason for our efforts and thus, was not able to receive our compassion. We must try again." The congregation collected an extremely large "love offering" that was forwarded to the woman. Such a response advanced the mission of the American Baptist Churches of Ohio and the First Baptist Church of Urbana, even in the midst of a disaster.

On another occasion, several pastors in the community who had been working hard at sending a signal of cooperation sponsored a community worship service in the midst of a drought. The worship service went a long way toward advancing the vision of unity held by the group of pastors. No matter what the disaster, there will be a way to advance God's vision as you respond.

### Advancing God's Vision

For a moment, reflect upon the ways that you might advance God's vision of your congregation amid your current crisis or as the next crisis dawns on the horizon. What is the vision for your church? Does it involve engaging people in ministry? If so, then a faithful leader of such an organization would find some way for the next crisis to call more people into ministry.

Does God's vision involve reaching out to a specific group of unchurched people? If so, the faithful leader in you will want to involve some of those targeted people in resolving the next crisis. Is the person who created or announced the crisis in your targeted group? Who, in your targeted group, has resources that can help you respond to the crisis?

Is God's vision related closely to your local community? If so, you as a faithful leader will want to find a way for your next crisis to fall under the umbrella of community involvement. You also will want to prepare for such a moment by building relationships with community leaders in advance.

Is spiritual growth and maturity your main emphasis? Given this parameter, the faithful leader would try to focus especially upon the spiritual components of the next crisis. She or he would couch the crisis in a theological framework and challenge other leaders to grow spiritually as a result of the dilemma.

Does God's vision involve a high level of discernment? How can you model that vision by spending some time discerning God's will during your next emergency? How might you call your members together to discern God's guidance prior to reacting to the next tense situation?

Whether the next crisis is related to your finances, to the health of one of your members, to the calling of a staff person, to a decision or ruling from one of your closely associated colleagues, or to the failure of a particular program or attempted outreach, consider ways to advance your vision in the midst of the crisis. Faithful leaders seek out ways to advance God's vision for their organization in the midst of bad news, by the way they respond to that news.

Do not abandon God's vision in the moment of a crisis. Use the vision to redeem the moment from potential disaster. Place a note card inscribed with your organization's vision statement by your phone in order to keep the vision at the surface during your next tense phone call. As we discussed earlier, the vision should be something easily understood and repeatable. But even the most memorable vision statements can be lost in the midst of an anxious phone call.

## Picking Up the Pieces of a Disaster

Advancing God's vision through a crisis is always Plan A. You will be happy to know that there is a Plan B. If no possible avenue for advancing the vision of your organization can be found, you certainly will want to deal responsibly with the crisis, but you will not want the crisis to build into a world of its own and detract from God's vision. Faithful leaders seek to contain crises that fall outside the realm of their current vision.

It will not be possible to advance the vision of your organization through every external crisis that impacts your congregation. You will not be able to create a kairos moment every time. What can you do with a crisis that is simply too large or too disconnected from your current vision to advance God's vision through the dilemma? Traditional wisdom usually promotes some form of dialogue among the damaged or conflicted parties of a potential crisis. Such dialogue is always appropriate at some future point, but the first appropriate response is to reestablish and rearticulate God's vision. In the midst of a potential catastrophe, the faithful leader either comes closer to God's vision as a result of the crisis or reassures the members that the current crisis will not derail them. I believe that attempted dialogue can actually be damaging if attempted prior to reestablishing the vision. That is because, in the heat of a crisis, dialogue is nearly impossible. When a crisis has been extremely hot, for a period of time you will not even be able to draw attention to the crisis and then build a bridge to your vision. No one will cross the bridge with you. It is sad, but still factual, that discussing the most recent crisis can be more stimulating for many than discussing news ways of advancing God's vision for your congregation.

In such situations, raise God's vision higher than it ever has been raised before. Following a debilitating crisis, people will look to the leader and give the leader every opportunity to abandon the vision. People who never bought into the vision fully will claim defeat for you. People will offer you a way out because they know that advancing the vision from this point will require even more work than before. But, if the vision has come from God, God will provide a way to get back on track with the vision, no matter what the nature of the most recent catastrophe.

## Maintaining Your Cool

It may not need to be said, but it is difficult to advance God's vision for your congregation in the midst of a crisis, if you are currently blowing a fuse. There are many ways of keeping your cool in the midst of crises. One way that was suggested to me several years ago is to build "crisis days" into your calendar. Advancing the vision of your congregation in the midst of a crisis will require "think time." The lack of it may limit your range of responses. One solution to this problem is to schedule in crisis days in order to allow you some time to ponder options regarding your latest crisis. The frequency of such days will obviously depend upon the frequency of major crises affecting your congregation.

Another technique that I used as a student was to write all deadlines for projects and papers one week early into my planner. This technique is similar to setting your wristwatch five minutes ahead. You will know the true time or the true deadline, but the psychological factor still works.

In the illustration above regarding the flood victim, it was difficult not to be intimidated or bullied into responding negatively to the woman's anger. It also was difficult to comprehend the range of emotions that the woman must have felt upon seeing all of her possessions on the sidewalk. Still, retaliations never win points and certainly never advance God's vision. Maintaining your cool goes a long way toward allowing you to advance the vision of your congregation in the midst of a crisis.

If everyone had the demeanor of my father, maintaining one's cool would not be an issue no matter what the crisis. One night during our church-bowling league, I happened to be substitute bowling next to the lane where my father's team was bowling. During the second of three games, he leaned over to me and whispered, "I'm not feeling well." That was the first time that I ever had heard my father report that he did not feel well. Even though such news was dramatic, it was quickly overshadowed by the hullabaloo of my father's third game. He had rolled a spare in the first frame and then proceeded to roll strikes. While the hope of a 300 game was no longer an option, watching someone roll the next ball after a string of five or six strikes was a sight to see. My dad ended up "striking out" (although a bad thing in baseball, it is a great thing in bowling). Immediately upon rolling the last ball, my dad said to me, "You drive home." That piece of instruction immediately told me that something was still very wrong with my father. While he tolerated my driving skills, he certainly did not relish them in the midst of an illness. I drove him straight to the hospital where they removed three kidney stones the next day. People wondered how my dad had been able to roll three games in the midst of the pain of kidney stones. My dad's response: "I figured out that if I rolled a strike, I only had to roll the ball once."

While I didn't receive that level of composure from my father, my own formula for keeping my cool in the midst of a crisis is this, "Expect three crises a day." I am not allowed to get upset until the fourth crisis. In my position, there often are three small crises on a daily basis. When the first one occurs, I respond, ""That's number one." Whenever I reach the statement, "That's number four," I try to take a little extra time before responding. After all, it is the first unexpected one of the day. I read a Psalm. I say a prayer. I call a friend. I take a walk. I get a cup of coffee. Then, I respond to the crisis and try to roll a strike. I try to advance God's vision even in the midst of the latest crisis. That's what faithful leaders do.

---

1   Stephen Covey, "Three Roles of the Leader," 150.

2   William Bridges, "Leading the De-Jobbed Organization," in The Leader of the Future, ed. Frances Hesselbein, Marshall Goldsmith, and Richard Beckard (San Francisco: Jossey-Bass Publishers, 1996), 13.

3   Judith Bardwick, "Peacetime Management and Wartime Leadership," in The Leader of the Future, ed. Frances Hesselbein, Marshall Goldsmith, and Richard Beckard (San Francisco: Jossey-Bass Publishers, 1996), 138.

4   Peter F. Drucker, "Not Enough Generals," 162.

# 5

## *CREATING KAIROS*

AS WE DISCOVERED IN THE LAST CHAPTER, KAIROS, a term indicating a time full of meaning and possibilities, is a needed word in today's culture and also in today's congregations. Society is searching for kairos moments, and the faithful leaders of today are discovering ways of delivering more kairos to a needy world.

There are two ways of adding kairos moments to your congregation. The first opportunity occurs in the midst of a crisis. When a crisis develops, faithful leaders look for ways to generate kairos moments within the calamity. They mobilize people to respond to the catastrophe. They challenge the membership to learn from the circumstances. They capitalize upon the fact that senses are heightened, hearts are poised for action, and willingness to get involved is at an all-time high. They advance the mission and vision of their congregation in the midst of the crisis. As we discovered in the last chapter, finding kairos in the midst of crisis events involves channeling people's energies toward positive results. That's what faithful leaders do.

But what about during times of peace and harmony: times of balanced budgets, a well-functioning staff team, and satisfied members? During plateau times, channeling energy into appropriate action is quickly replaced by concerns over lethargy and lassitude. How does a leader striving to be faithful create kairos amid a sea of apathy? How do you create meaningful moments when there is little or no energy available? Some might suggest creating a new crisis in which to mobilize the people or crying "catastrophe" over nominal obstacles. Creating a false sense of urgency can be a successful method for leaders. But it is not a method that faithful leaders promote. Faithful leaders do not succumb to such "wag the dog" philosophies. During times of complacency within a group or congregation, faithful leaders create kairos moments by taking their leadership core to the next level of development and then trusting God to supply the next great challenge.

God cannot resist a willing worker or a motivated band of people. "For the eyes of the Lord range throughout the entire earth, to strengthen those whose heart is true to him" (2 Chronicles 16:9). God hunts for the "Here am I's." To whom much is given much is required and, in turn, much will be offered in the way of opportunities. During times of satisfaction, faithful leaders learn how to facilitate development within a group to such an extent that the group becomes ready for a challenge larger than the previous one. As faithful leaders prepare their memberships to receive God's next great challenge, God prepares to intersect the paths of those who hold empty cups with those whose cups are full of cold, fresh water. Just as Peter and Cornelius received dual identical visions, the same God today prepares both the giver and the receiver to benefit from the impending interaction.

Once God does supply the next great challenge, the leader may discover that the leadership core is not as trained as previously perceived or may encounter new congregational crises amid some who are resistant to change. But crises created from within the organization as a result of growing pains are very different from crises created outside the organization to which the congregational leadership seeks to respond. The last chapter dealt with responding to changes that primarily arise on the outside of the congregation. This chapter challenges the leader to change the congregation from the inside out. Both sets of activities are aimed at claiming more of God's available kairos. In the last chapter the goal was to channel the already present level of energy into worthwhile pursuits. This chapter will lead to an increased level of energy within the congregation as norms are challenged and learning soars. Faithful leaders learn how to build more kairos moments into the life of the congregation they are leading. Sometimes kairos can be created from crises. Other times it must be built from the ground up. Building kairos can be risky. It requires that the leader pay significant attention to moods, atmosphere, and timing, lest the created tensions escalate beyond a manageable level.

## Battling Inertia

In the last chapter, we realized that the world is dramatically changing. Thus, at first glance, it would seem odd to seek to add to the superfluity of change in today's society. But when faced with the problem of inertia rather than the problem of rapid change, it is necessary to create some unrest in order to garner enough energy to implement God's next great challenge. Leaders avoid potential crises down the road by encouraging change within the stagnant parts of a congregation. There are not many organizational factors more difficult to deal with than rapid change. An overabundance of inertia, however, is one of them. In other words, the only thing more difficult than responding to change is realizing that you should have changed and did not. Nancy Ammerman's research suggests, "Congregations that do not try new programs and new forms of outreach ... are not likely to survive past the life spans of their current members."[1]

Do not underestimate the power of inertia. Rapid change makes one feel as if one were in a dust storm. Inertia is more like quicksand. No matter where and how the leader tries to move, the outcome is simply to drown more deeply in the mire. Ammerman explains the problems of inertia, "Even when there are no official barriers, cultural norms defining the legitimate range of activity constrain the imaginations of organizational leaders. To attempt some kinds of adaptation would require reinterpreting the organization to its constituents.... For all these reasons, the most common response to change is inertia."[2]

People do not like to change. Change involves getting rid of something old and accepting something new. Saying good-bye to the old is like a death, and most church leaders are well aware of the potentially strapping emotions associated with grieving over the lost, and in this case, perceived paradise lost. Battling resistance to a new vision or a new program is not for the timid.

Jesus challenged the disciples to cast their nets on the other side of the boat. Many proven church leaders do not want to do this, not for fear of unknown waters, but for fear of known and unwanted waters! They think they know what is on the other side of the boat ... the sea of change inhabited by the Loch Ness monster of resistance! For good reason many leaders choose not to go there, not to cast their nets into revolutionary waters. Yet faithful leaders find a way to respond appropriately to the pangs of inertia. Faithful leaders learn how to battle inertia because they know that sustained inertia will eventually lead to a lack of growth for the members and certainly a lack of interest from potential members outside the congregation. Bardwick explains, "By definition, leaders lead change. When life is orderly, tasks are predictable, and most things are going well, people neither want nor need much leadership."[3] Leaders lead change. Faithful leaders find ways to create kairos.

Even though battling inertia is inevitable when seeking to change a congregation from the inside out, detecting inertia is not quite so easy. Inertia can sometimes be disguised by a flurry of activity, called work avoidance. A congregation characterized by *work avoidance* is one in which the members are working hard at avoiding change rather than dealing with change. Heifetz explains, "People fail to adapt because of the distress provoked by the problem and the changes it demands. They resist the pain, anxiety, or conflict ... blaming authority, scapegoating, externalizing the enemy, denying the problem, jumping to conclusions ... These patterns of response to disequilibria are called work avoidance mechanisms."[4] Without realizing it, people may expend more effort battling change than they would if they embraced the change.

For the majority of members within any congregation, inertia represents the traditional way of doing things. They do things a certain way precisely because they have been done that way the previous time, and the time before that, and … you get the picture. Clinching inertia should never be equated with a poor work ethic or a lack of commitment. Quite the contrary. Ammerman discovered that nonadapting congregations have far higher levels of commitment than do adapting ones. "If commitment is measured in terms of regular attendance and giving high percentages of their personal incomes, the members of declining congregations are, on average, more committed."[5] Faithful leaders understand that no matter how committed the core leadership group is to the next great idea many in their congregation would rather maintain the present course than try out a new innovation. Promoting change when people prefer inertia can lead to chaos. With a few faithful leadership principles, however, it also can lead to kairos.

## Awaiting the Next Great Challenge

Many of the skills presented in chapter one regarding discerning a vision from God can be incorporated into the process of discovering God's next great challenge for your congregation. God's next great challenge may be the unveiling of the vision itself, or it may incorporate one component of the vision, or it may involve dealing with a conflict or problem that is currently sapping all of the available energy, making it impossible to deal with God's vision until the problem is addressed. God's next great challenge for your congregation may not be brand new. Merton P. Strommen reminds us that an innovation may either be:

• The application of a new idea in an old setting, OR
• The application of an old idea in a new setting.[6]

Taking time to discern God's direction for your congregation is much more important than the magnitude of the ideas that surface. Any successful leader could present one good idea after another to occupy the time of a particular group or congregation. But a faithful leader takes time to discern God's will. Patience sets faithful leaders apart from successful leaders. Faithful leaders go beyond the world's ideas of success and derive their satisfaction from serving God rather than peers. Just because a project is successful does not necessarily mean that the project was God's choice for your congregation.

Leaders should never be too anxious to launch the next great challenge, especially when the leader perceives that the group is getting ahead of God's plan. When Moses was in the midst of a thirsty people, God allowed Moses simply to strike a rock in order to produce fresh water for the Israelites. But remember what God instructed Moses to name the place: "He called the place Massah [test] and Meribah [find fault], because the Israelites quarreled and tested the Lord" (Exodus 17:7). God was faithful to meet the needs of the Israelites, as God has promised to do for us during wilderness times, but God reminds us that the ultimate preference is for us to have a higher level of patience. Later in the story, striking the rock is actually cited as one of the reasons why Moses did not enter the Promised Land. "'Because you did not trust in me, to show my holiness before the eyes of the Israelites, therefore you shall not bring this assembly into the land that I have given them. These are the waters of Meribah, where the people … quarreled with the Lord" (Numbers 20:12–13). Faithful leaders look to God to supply the next challenge. They also look to God to supply the timing.

## Promoting Member Development

In the absence of putting out fires within their organization, leaders are afforded time for team building, reflection, personal goal setting, performance appraisal, organizational development, and skill enhancement. In the midst of a crisis, there is no shortage of energy. In the absence of conflict, however, leaders need to exercise the cheerleader role, encouraging the members to strive for maximum development.

One way for leaders to promote member development is to increasingly raise expectations for the membership. In my previous position as a local church pastor, I would consistently say, "If the members of this church are not closer to God now than the previous year, then something is wrong." As a pastor I tried to consistently lift up the expectation that every member would regularly grow in faith. Other leaders may choose additional phrases, such as, "If every member does not know more about the Bible … ," or, "If every member has not grown in the application of the Scriptures … ," or, "If every member has not developed a greater sense of confidence in carrying out one of the ministries of the congregation.…"

Such statements should not be made without supplying multiple opportunities for the membership to achieve your expectations, whether they be drawing closer to God, learning more about the Scriptures, or developing ministry skills. Pastors or group leaders set the stage for lifelong learning by continuing to read material that stretches their minds and inspires their hearts. Such experiences will naturally spill over into the lives of the membership. Calling upon the assistance of outside consultants or experts, trained in such topics as team building, group dynamics, goal setting, etc., can also be an excellent way to promote member development during the more peaceful times of a group's existence. Further ideas for member development also are presented in chapter six.

George Bullard, a well-known church consultant, offers a statistic that may influence some leaders to think about the way that they promote member development. Bullard recently explained that the distance between the development level of the core leaders within a congregation and the development level of the body of members within the same congregation remains fairly constant over time. Thus, one way of advancing the development of the entire membership of your congregation is to consistently challenge your core leadership to stay on the cutting edge.

Faithful leaders expect that God may supply the next great challenge at any moment. They do not wait passively for God to supply the next great challenge. They continue to prepare themselves for action, knowing that God cannot resist a prepared and committed group of faithful leaders.

## Sensing Readiness

Faithful leaders do not simply create change; they search for potential moments of kairos, moments that will forever be full of meaning. At some point in every instructor's day, there will be a teachable moment. The good teachers learn to recognize such instants. Both leaders and teachers look for moments of readiness. Faithful leaders learn to recognize kairos opportunities. Strommen's research reveals five characteristics of a congregation with a readiness to respond to innovation:

- an attitude of openness
- a listening stance
- a strong mission focus
- a motivation to improve what is being done
- a minimum of internal conflict[7]

I believe that faithful leaders who have sensed a need to work toward God's next great challenge within their congregation would do well to understand and work toward Strommen's five organizational characteristics of readiness to change. Several of Strommen's characteristics will come very naturally for faithful leaders. First of all, faithful leaders will naturally work to create an attitude of openness within the congregation. By definition, a faithful leader is one who remains open to God. Faithful leaders trust in God as their source of power and amazement. It would be difficult to remain open to God and not also remain open to God's ability to do a wonderful new thing everyday. Second, remaining open to God's guidance logically leads to a listening stance on the part of the faithful leader. Faithful leaders learn, not only to listen to God, but also to those they are leading. Third, a strong mission focus will come naturally for faithful leaders because faithful leaders are unsurprisingly more concerned about ministry than maintenance, more concerned about missions than budgets.

Strommen's fourth characteristic, promoting a desire within the organization to constantly improve on what is being done, is a trait of all leaders who strive for excellence. It certainly should be something that faithful leaders, who desire to go beyond success, advance as well. Never underestimate this factor. No leader, no matter how charismatic, can bring about significant change within the congregation if its members do not desire improvement.

As has been shown thus far, four of the five organizational elements of readiness uncovered by Strommen's research should come quite naturally for faithful leaders. Strommen's fifth element, however, may not come quite so naturally. Possibly the biggest mistake that leaders make in not correctly sensing an opportune moment for advancing an innovation or creating a kairos moment, is promoting change when there is already a high level of internal conflict within the congregation. Seeking to implement God's next great challenge for your congregation will increase the level of conflict. If there already is a high level of internal strife, the congregation may not be able to handle the added stress.

When I came to my present position, I knew that there were four or five major organizational problems to solve. I also knew that it was unlikely that any significant internal kairos opportunities would surface until most of the existing problems had been addressed. Sometimes leaders mistakenly point to conflict as evidence they are being faithful to God. While Jesus often stirred up the status quo, there were moments of great harmony among the disciples. Too much internal conflict may signal a need to wage peace rather than an opportune time to promote change.

# Volunteering for Wilderness Duty

Making a commitment to create kairos from within rather than simply respond to crises outside the organization will not come without trepidation. Times of searching for kairos are similar to wilderness times for organizations. Wilderness times do not present easy roads. Wilderness times are times where God consistently meets the physical needs of the group or individual, but also consistently challenges the group or individual to deeper dependence upon God. Wilderness duty requires an active search for meaning as well as deliberate acts of preparation before entering into the Promised Land. Faithful leaders engaged in kairos hunting may take comfort in the fact that God will meet the needs of their followers while in the wilderness, but at the same time they will be stressed by the remembrance that the Israelite leaders possessed no shortage of grumbling from their followers while they searched for new meanings. This may be the reason that so very few of the leaders in our churches volunteer for wilderness duty.

One strategy that can help appease the grumbling is to point out that a search for new meanings does not imply that the old meanings or methods were wrong. "Looking for a new direction does not imply that the directions of the past were wrong, but *merely* questions their fitness for the present." Allen likens the search for new meaning to a shipwreck. "The journey is the same, the destination unchanged, but the direction finder at the core of our efforts may need renewal at such crossroads."[8] Building upon, rather than discounting the past, is a strategy that can assist the creation of kairos moments. You will discover other strategies for creating kairos in the paragraphs below. These strategies can help you advance a new vision, promote certain aspects of that vision, or address problem areas in order to ready a group for a new vision—all of which lead to the creation of more kairos amidst the *chronos,* or ordinary portions, of our lives.

# Additional Strategies for Creating Kairos

In bringing about change within an organization there is a right way and a wrong way. Basically, one method embraces strategy and planning and the other does not. (I'll let you guess which is my preferred method.)

Formulating a plan to implement God's next great challenge for your congregation will go a long way toward ensuring its acceptance by the membership. I am convinced that many of God's plans are foiled, not by a lack of enthusiasm or a lack of commitment on the part of the leadership, but simply from a lack of planning ahead. Below, I have listed several methods for implementing change. The methods and strategies described in this chapter may be applied to implementing the next great challenge that God has provided for your church. If the changes are implemented in an attitude of prayer and with sensitivity to the readiness of the congregation, they can lead to a kairos moment. The seven strategies listed below may be used to implement a new vision, a new idea, a new program, or a new technology. The emphasis here is upon process rather than content.

### Create Task Forces
Some call them ad hoc groups, others holding environments, still others guiding coalitions. But whatever they are called, Strommen claims the following, "I believe task forces are the key to innovation."[9] I have to agree. Forming a new group to design and implement God's next great project for your congregation will be one of the keys to its victorious realization. Kotter suggests four key elements in putting together the kind of team that can direct a change effort:

1. Position power: Getting enough key players on board
2. Expertise: Ensuring that all points of view are represented
3. Credibility: Members with strong reputations can add to the integrity of announcements
4. Leadership: Include proven leaders[10]

Forming a specialty group to develop and guide God's next great project provides the necessary insulation so that the group will not be burned by the heat caused by the rumors associated with a new idea. Appointing a task force buys some time for some of the members in your group to give their best thinking to the project at hand. It also allows you to put together a specific team for the specific issue at hand. If task forces become a regular part of the way that you operate as a leader, then, over time several of the members of your congregation will have an opportunity to serve on such groups.

## Involve First, Announce Second

The old way of getting things done is to announce that you plan to do something, couple it with a plea for help, and expect people to follow. The old method involves a two-step process: You announce the goal and expect the means to follow. That method doesn't work very well anymore, especially for controversial ideas. With the increased emphasis upon personal experience, the new way of getting things done is to engage people in an activity and then allow everything else to emerge from the group. This new method involves a four-step process. First of all, you recognize that there may be a variety of reasons for working toward a goal *(diverse ends)*. If you gathered a group together at this point to discuss all of those reasons, however, they might choose to meet as a committee for an entire year or two prior to taking any action! In fact, someone recently reported at a church leadership conference that churches with evangelism committees are not growing as fast as those without evangelism committees! Committees can be the death of ideas.

The second step of this new process (actually the first action step) involves *(common means)*. Engage the people in a common activity.

For example, rather than announcing that you would like for your group to become more spiritual this year, simply spend the first ten minutes of your next several meetings in prayer. Make sure that the prayers are insightful and inspiring. Prepare the prayers in advance. Consider the specific spiritual needs of your individual members and your group as a whole. After a few meetings, believe it or not, someone will announce your goal for you *(common ends)*. You will discover that if someone in your group surfaces your goal rather than you, the ownership of the idea will be much greater. Tex Sample, a sociologist, suggests that the inside leader should always avoid appearing to be the expert. Rather than yourself, allow someone in your group to say something like, "During these last few weeks, I have really come closer to God through your prayers," or, "During these last few weeks, our committee has grown deeper in our faith." Whatever phrase someone uses that you can live with, reply, "Yes, I'm glad to hear you say that ... that has been my goal for the last few weeks." Once you reveal your original intention, someone else is sure to add, "Well, if that is the goal, I have a few other ideas that might help" *(diverse means)*.[11] Before you know it, every member of the group is pitching in ideas to achieve a goal owned by your entire committee.

*Summary:*
- Diverse ends
- Common means
- Common ends
- Diverse means

### Appeal to the Four People Groups

Nutrition experts once boasted of the four food groups. Church consultants discuss the four people groups that can be found in nearly every congregation. Ed Peirce, a church-conflict management consultant, first introduced me to the four people groups. I have tested his theory with many congregations, and it always provides the congregation with some new insights. According to the theory, nearly every congregation will be characterized by four distinct groups, each one possessing a different need. The first group of people identify with the founders of the congregation. They have a need to know who is in charge of the congregation. Most people mistakenly think that this group has a need to be in charge themselves, which can be the case, but more often, they simply want to know who is responsible for decision making. Their ultimate concern is that the charter of the organization, or its original founding purposes, will continue.

The second group identifies with a particular program or ministry of the church, such as the choir or the youth group. They have a need to know that the particular ministry that meant so much to them over the years will continue in some form. The first two groups are task oriented. The last two groups, which often have joined since the arrival of the current pastor, are relationship oriented. The third group identifies with a particular small group such as a Sunday-school class or a mission circle. For this group, the majority of their friendships are contained in the particular small group. They need to know that their social network will not be threatened. The difference between group two and group three is that group two's needs center on a particular function of the church, while group three's needs center on a social network. The fourth group consists of new members or new Christians. They obviously have a need to be mentored, discipled, or assimilated into the life of the church. If this need is not met, they will soon be gone.

In promoting a new idea, a new vision, a new program, etc., it is important to keep in mind the four distinct needs of these people groups. While there may be other people in your congregation that do not easily fall into one of these four groups, if conflict surfaces in response to a new idea, it is most likely to surface among these groups. Thus, it is a good idea for the task force overseeing the design and implementation of the new project to brainstorm about how the new project may affect these four groups as well as how the primary need within each group can still be met. WARNING: Skipping this step may be hazardous to your leadership. If this step is skipped, proceed at your own risk. You may soon be calling upon the services of a professional Christian mediator!

### Place the Idea into a Theological Context

Spend some time in a task force meeting answering the question, "What Bible story does this project spur in our minds?" For a church, it is extremely important to ground any new project in a theological base. Connecting the challenge to a Bible story can be an excellent way of beginning to form a theological base for the idea. Ask the group, "What biblical story does this new challenge remind you of? What biblical characters faced similar circumstances? What biblical dilemmas might be similar to the ones that lie in store for us?" Seek to discover how the chosen biblical story influences your current project.

When a congregation fails to keep up with the times, by allowing outdated programs and projects to prevail, such lack of forethought can lead to financial crises and membership crises. Maneuvering a congregation into position to accept God's next great challenge cannot be done without a lot of hard work and an ability to dispense hope for the future. There is no greater source of hope than God's Word. Dispensing hope often involves creating moments of mystery and symbols of significance for people to hang on to as they dream of a better future for their congregation. Faithful leaders challenge the critical human mass within a congregation to take a bold posture that can faithfully navigate resistant waters in order to sail God's new vessel for their congregation.

If no theological basis can be found, maybe God is not the source of the project! If God authored the project, God has the ability to assist your group with the placement of the project in theological context. Recalling similar biblical stories or principles will always provide additional insights for designing, implementing, and promoting the project.

### Plan Equal Amounts of Time for Design and Implementation

How long did it take your congregation to approve the new idea? Count the entire amount of time from the idea's inception until final approval. Even include those parking-lot conversations prior to the official conversations that may not have taken place until months later. How long did the process take? Three weeks? Three months? Three years? Whatever your answer, the overseeing task force should design at least as long a time for the implementation of the idea. That may sound like an extreme amount of time, but many good ideas get lost, even after their approval, because the overseeing group did not design a long-enough implementation period for the idea. Implementing an idea requires good strategy. It also requires time for the idea to become embedded in the life of your congregation. Do not rush your implementation ideas.

Plan enough implementation strategies to equal the design and execution periods. Naturally, a building-program task force will require months of work prior to introducing their final plan to the congregation. In the same vein, the implementation of that project will take a considerable amount of time to complete. Launching a fellowship program for seniors may take considerably less time to design. If that is the case, then its implementation phase also can be shortened. Keep in mind that an implementation is not complete until the new idea has been absorbed into the lifeblood of the congregation. A new idea will not stick until it has been woven into the congregation's fabric.

### Endorse Primary Planning

Did you hear about the pastor who was leaving town? He strolled into the local pet store and put in an order for 150 mice, 300 roaches, and 10,000 carpenter ants.

"My, but that is an unusual request!" came the startled reply of the pet storeowner.

"Well, you see," said the pastor. "I'm moving out of the parsonage of First Church in town and the trustees instructed me, 'Leave the place as you found it.'"

That is a crude story, but it illustrates primary planning quite well. The pastor of First Church had a *primary interest* in that parsonage. Obviously, the trustees had only a *secondary interest* in the parsonage!

When planning an event, designing a task force, or implementing a program, be sure to include people with a primary interest in the project, rather than merely a secondary interest.

### Listen and Persuade in Equal Amounts

During the first half of the implementation phase of the project, attention will usually be focused upon selling the idea or promoting the merits of the project. Gilbert Rendle in his book, *Leading Change in the Congregation,* suggests that at some point during the implementation phase attention should shift away from persuasion toward a more listening posture.[12] At some point, people no longer resist the merits of an idea; they begin to resist "being changed."

What usually happens at this point of resistance is that the implementing group goes back to the brainstorming board to produce several more reasons why the challenge is a good one. Such efforts, however, only serve to make the other members of the congregation feel even more as if the new challenge is being thrust upon them, causing them to become even more resistant. The greater the effort to convince, the greater the effort to resist! If someone is no longer objecting to the idea, but merely resisting having the idea forced upon them, then we can only expect increased resistance from increased persuasion! The only workable strategy at this point is to truly listen to people who are resisting being changed. Their objections may already have been covered or they may not appear to be rational. But for whatever reason, the people do not feel that they have been heard. The only way that such a project can proceed at that point is if leaders truly listen to the ones still objecting.

## Searching for More Chronos

Creating kairos is more about timing than it is about time, more about wit than it is about skills, and more about prayer than it is about might. Mistakenly, even since biblical times, people have thought that the answer to life was more chronos, rather than more kairos. "If there were only a few more hours in the day!" Such laments are not new. People have seldom understood that kairos is actually the answer to a request for more chronos. Nicodemus asked, "Can one enter a second time into the mother's womb and be born?" (John 3:4). Martha pleaded for more chronos by asking for her sister to help her with the preparations. Even Jesus, expressing his humanity, asked, "'Father, if you are willing, remove this cup from me'" (Luke 22:42), but settled in on the kairos of the moment.

We do not need more chronos. We need more kairos. We need to discover ways to create more kairos moments. We need to faithfully prepare the congregation so that it will be in a position to embrace God's next great challenge when it arrives. Look, over the horizon. There it is now!

---

1 Nancy Tatom Ammerman, Congregation and Community (New Brunswick, N. J.: Rutgers University Press, 1997), 323.

2 Ibid. 63.

3 Judith Bardwick, "Peacetime Management and Wartime Leadership," in The Leader of the Future, 131.

4 Heifetz, Leadership without Easy Answers, 37.

5 Ammerman, 327.

6 Merton P. Strommen, The Innovative Church: Seven Steps to Positive Change in Your Congregation (Minneapolis: Augsburg, 1997), 16.

7 Ibid., 19.

8 Allen, Crossroads in Christian Growth, 38.

9 Strommen, 42.

10 Kotter, John, Leading Change.

11 For a more detailed description of this theory, refer to Woods, We've Never Done It Like This Before, 83–90.

12 Gilbert Rendle, Leading Change in the Congregation (Bethesda, Md.: Alban Institute, 1998), 119.

# 6

## *MAKING MENTORS*

**T**HERE ARE SOME THINGS THAT CANNOT BE learned from books. Passing the written test to obtain a learner's permit will not teach someone how to drive. Subscribing to *Golf Digest* is not enough to learn the game of golf. One cannot learn to design a car by taking an engineering class. Books may assist gardeners, but by themselves, cannot make someone a gardener. One can learn about the stages of dying from a textbook, but one must learn how to show compassion to a dying person by spending time with that person.

Similarly, some aspects of leadership must be learned through experience. You can learn about the mechanics of delivering a speech or a sermon in a classroom but must learn from experience how to handle unexpected interruptions and congregational feedback. You can read about conflict management techniques, but must practice those skills in order to become a leader who can also work through conflict. You can read about various problem-solving techniques, but only through solving simple problems can you learn how to solve major problems. Successful leaders know that some aspects of leadership must either be learned by experience or received from a trainer.

Faithful leaders even take the learning process a step beyond training and experience. Faithful leaders know that any aspect of leadership that would best be learned from experience or training would be even better learned from a mentor. Faithful leaders learn certain aspects of leadership from mentors. They also know that mentoring others is a necessary part of faithful leadership.

When we think of leadership, we usually think of leaders, not leadership books. Pondering leadership brings to mind people who have made a difference in society. We think of people who have been so singularly focused that they mobilized others to join their cause and compromised nothing in achieving their goal. When we think of becoming leaders ourselves, we often think of emulating other great leaders. Wouldn't it be wonderful to spend time with Billy Graham, Marian Wright Edelman, Millard Fuller, or Mother Teresa, or to have known and been directed by Martin Luther King Jr., Helen Barrett Montgomery, Albert Einstein, or Amelia Earhardt? Spending time with admired leaders is a great way of learning about leadership.

All effective leaders have both learned from other leaders and learned how to develop other leaders. Leadership training and development is an indispensable part of successful leadership. Christian leaders, however, are not focused on success. They are focused on faithfulness. Faithful leaders do not just train other leaders. They mentor potential leaders. Although many organizations, both religious and secular, encourage mentoring, for Christian congregations and organizations, mentoring is the fundamental form of leadership development. No better example of mentoring can be found than the example of Jesus mentoring the disciples. As Christ's followers, we are compelled to mentor others today in order to advance God's mission. Mentoring is the Christian way of developing leaders.

Jesus provided the definitive example of mentoring when he spent three years training the disciples to carry on his ministry. Jesus did not just train the disciples; he spent time with them. He ate with them. He traveled with them. He encouraged them. He chastised them. He challenged them. He supported them. He did not just give of himself, he gave his whole self. He did not just pass along the extra, he passed along the best. He did not just teach skills, he taught a philosophy. He did not merely call the disciples to a task. He called them to a lifestyle. He gave them everything that they needed to continue the ministry. That is not merely training. That is mentoring.

Mentoring is a skill that involves more than passing along a set of information. The modern term *mentor* actually dates all the way back to Greek mythology. Odysseus had to be away from home for an extended period of time. He engaged Mentor to educate and look after his son during his absence. Mentoring involves giving of our entire selves for the education and instruction of others. Mentoring involves more than teaching a set of skills or tasks, it takes us beyond training.

## Mentoring vs. Training

Mentoring differs from training in some very fundamental ways. First of all, mentoring shares the whole person with another, not just a portion of oneself. Mentoring involves revealing the very best of whom we are with someone else, in hopes that the mentee may someday reveal the very best of who he or she is with another. Mentoring involves more than demonstrating a skill. In mentoring, values and viewpoints are shared. Stories from the past and mutual experiences are more a part of a mentoring relationship than graphs, charts, manuals, and textbooks.

Mentors do not develop an agenda for mentoring the mentee. Even in situations where the mentor and mentee have regular meeting times, preset agendas are usually impractical because the mentor does not know what to draw upon until the needs of the mentee surface. And the needs of the mentee may change quite frequently. In a mentoring situation, the relationship is more important than a particular set of tasks to be learned. In fact, many mentors express the fact that they did not know that they were mentoring someone else or being mentored by another until they were well into the mentoring relationship.

While I encourage leaders to be intentional about mentoring relationships, it is true that they are often difficult to distinguish from friendship relationships, especially early in the process. When the mentor makes a commitment to fostering development of the whole person, this is the beginning of the mentoring relationship.

A second way that mentoring differs from training is that in a mentoring relationship the needs of the mentee are paramount to the needs of the mentor. In a training relationship on the other hand, the skill that the trainer has been assigned to teach takes precedent over the needs of the trainee. The needs of the trainee may affect or even inhibit the training process, but are still secondary to the goal of learning what the trainer is trying to teach.

In a mentoring relationship there are good reasons to support the fact that the needs of the mentee should be the primary focus. For example, it is impossible to bring about the best in another person while ignoring factors that may be inhibiting the person from being what God wants him or her to be. A good mentor will bring to the surface the needs and nuances of the mentee by asking open-ended questions in a variety of categories. The needs of the mentee actually shape the information that is passed along to the mentee. In a training relationship, the trainee is responsible for integrating the newly learned skill into his or her repertoire. In a mentoring relationship, integration of new and old skills is a frequent topic of conversation and can be one of the best gifts given to the mentee.

Training and mentoring also have different bottom lines. The bottom line of training is to encourage the trainee to be *the* best at a particular skill. Being the best is relative only to the group that one is in. The bottom line of mentoring is to encourage the mentee to reach the potential of what God wants him or her to be. Mentoring is not about encouraging someone else to be the best among a group of peers. It is about encouraging someone to be his or her best as measured against God's potential for that person. The difference may be subtle, but it is essential to understanding the mentoring relationship. Training is concerned with helping someone master something, and thus, can quickly become competition oriented. Mentoring's goal is to assist an individual in discovering what God wants for him or her and then to encourage the mentee to become that person. It is about discerning God's role for the person in the group, the congregation, or in life.

A final way that training and mentoring differ is that, in training the trainee is accountable to the trainer, while a mentoring relationship involves mutual accountability. At the end of a training session, the trainee is often invited to give feedback regarding the training session. But such feedback is usually processed in solitude by the trainer. A good mentoring relationship will provide constant feedback between mentor and mentee about the relationship. In a mentoring relationship, the mentor also is encouraged to learn from the mentee. While the mentee learns about how to juggle multiple tasks, how to respond to dilemmas, how to prioritize, etc., the mentor is able to witness and learn from the implementation of old skills in new settings. The mentee also is encouraged to share new insights with the mentor. Experience may be the best teacher, but insights not tainted with experience can provide a fresh perspective. The participants in a mentoring relationship share both learning and accountability.

## The Tasks of a Mentor

I believe that the first and most important task of a Christian mentor is to display the fruits of the Spirit in the mentoring relationship. What a mentee needs most from a mentor is to witness the fruits of the Spirit being lived out within the same vocational context into which the mentee is being called. Love, joy, peace, patience, kindness, goodness, faithfulness, gentleness, and self-control are better displayed rather than dictated. Christians are called to practice the fruits of the Spirit on a daily basis, each one. Yes, we will fail on a daily basis, but we are not allowed to write any of those that we regularly break permanently off of our list! The fruits are not like the gifts of the Spirit. We cannot say, "Well since I do not have the gift of compassion, I can be an ogre on a regular basis!" Practicing the fruits of the Spirit is more important in a mentoring relationship than in any other relationship. You don't learn to how to practice the fruits of the Spirit in a book or a lecture; you learn them by experience and example.

We are all called to practice what we preach. That is because people will believe our actions, our facial expressions, even the tone of our words over the content of the message. The good intentions of a mentor will be destroyed more quickly by a lack of demonstrating the fruits of the Spirit than by any other influence. The number-one role of the mentor relates to integrity. Integrity is more easily assimilated from a mentoring relationship than it is acquired from hard work. Mentors should relate their difficult decisions and their struggles with ethical choices with those whom they are mentoring. For it is in this manner that mentees will learn how to make ethical decisions of their own. Integrity is an important quality to display for those who are watching leaders and even more important for those whom we are mentoring.

The second task of a mentor is to see in others what they cannot see themselves. Dostoevsky once said, "To love someone is to see them as the person God intended them to be rather than the person that they are." As mentors learn to love their mentees, they begin to see in each person, potential beyond the comprehension of the person being mentored. Nearly every person mentored proclaims at some point, "My mentor saw in me something that I could not yet see." Self-esteem comes slowly, especially in new arenas of skill. Esteem from another often precedes self-esteem. It is perhaps for this reason that our mentors see us accomplishing certain tasks far more quickly and easily than we ever thought possible. "Coaches and teachers can often see what parents cannot see, because at times, *they* are too close to the situation."[1] In a similar manner, mentors learn to see in others something that they cannot see themselves.

One particular mentor that I had in my doctoral program in Educational Research asked me one Friday, "What are you doing this weekend?"

I had learned to answer such questions with brutal honesty. "I have plans on Friday evening with my wife, but other than that I am free," I replied.

"Will you have time to do a little reading?"

"Yes."

"If you do the reading, you could earn a little extra money next week."

What grad student wouldn't want to earn some extra money? I quickly agreed to the reading.

"Take this box home with you and come prepared on Monday to serve with me as an external evaluator of a gifted and talented program." The box contained twenty-four reports of previous external evaluation projects in which my mentor had participated. I was glad that I had been honest about my plans for the weekend, for my mentor gave me enough reading to consume all of the free time that I had reported to him. We had discussed several of the cases, and I had completed the necessary courses for the particular statistical skills required, but I didn't think that I was ready to serve as a consultant with him. But I did. And my mentor had little doubt that I was ready. The case also presented new opportunities to gain more out of our mentoring relationship. Mentors have a way of sensing readiness before mentees.

The third role of a mentor is to help the mentee develop her or his main gift needed for the task at hand. Sometimes this involves assisting the mentee with the development of a life-long personal mission statement as described in the third chapter. Other times this involves assisting the mentee with the development of a new set of skills centered on a common thread. Not only are mentors able to see potential that the mentees themselves cannot see, they often are able to discern vocational desires or personal mission desires not yet realized by their mentees. As I look back upon my life, every time that I was ready to expand my career goals or apply my personal mission statement to a new arena, God provided a mentor to help guide me through that new phase of life. In every case, the mentor helped me focus more clearly upon the main task at hand. Mentors, better than anyone else, can help clear away the clutter, scuffle away the excuses, and funnel down the faculties into a clear sense of short-term purpose.

# Developing a Team through Mentoring

Since mentoring is the primary means of leadership development for Christians, many Christian leaders utilize mentoring skills in order to build a collegial staff team of workers or volunteers capable of accomplishing God's mission set before them.

### Beyond Equipping

The success model of leadership development focuses upon the leader as the trainer, and in many congregational success models, as the equipper. But the faithful leader recognizes that at some point, training and equipping must end in order to allow the mentoring process to encourage the mentee to develop his or her ministry beyond the skill level of the leader. The role of the trainer or equipper is to help the trainee master a particular skill. The ultimate goal of the trainee is to learn to perform the skill as well as the trainer. The role of the mentor is to help mentees develop their particular ministries to the best of their abilities. Because of the unique background of each mentee, the mentor trusts that God has some ministry task in mind for the mentee that the mentee can perform more effectively than anyone else, including the mentor.

An equipping style of ministry is hierarchical. A mentoring style of ministry is heterarchical. Kennon Callahan explains the dangers of a hierarchical or top-down approach to leadership. The dangers are particularly prevalent within the church.

> Some have adopted a philosophy of hierarchicalism. A philosophy of life based on a hierarchy tends to create an understanding of leadership that focuses upon "being the boss." The more drastic the hierarchical perspective, the more readily the boss's understanding of leadership progresses to that of benevolent, authoritarian dictator.... The more successful the boss becomes in acquiring power, the more convinced this person becomes of a hierarchical philosophy of life.... It is not accidental that this perspective *always* builds a caste system in the church.[2]

Mentoring strives to develop each person's ability beyond that of the leader. In this sense, mentoring is actually reverse hierarchical.

As a pastor of a local congregation, I often tried to equip new Christians with ministry skills. But, at some point, I stopped training and trusted God to couple needed spiritual gifts with the person's natural abilities and background in order to perform his or her ministry better than I could perform that ministry. In an equipping relationship, it will always be assumed that the equipper knows more than the one being equipped. In a mentoring relationship, it is assumed that the mentee will develop his or her particular ministry beyond the level of the mentor, because the mentor will not possess the same set of abilities as the mentee. Nancy Ammerman discovered that pastors who were viewed as having strong leadership skills also were devoted to strong lay participation.[3] Faithful leaders and faithful pastors recognize that having others on their staff team or members within their parish who can perform certain aspects of ministry better than they can, is a reason to celebrate, not a cause for alarm.

The goal of faithful mentoring is to encourage persons within your congregation to develop the best of who they are in hopes that the very best of who they are will better help the congregation accomplish God's mission. In order for this model to work with minimal conflict, the members also must understand that their role is to strengthen the congregation in order that it might better accomplish God's mission, rather than to sustain his or her particular position. Noer calls this the "paradox of freedom." "This is perhaps the most profound learning, which I call the *paradox of freedom. The paradox of job security* is that when people choose to stay for the right reasons (the work and the customer [and in our context—the accomplishment of God's mission]), as opposed to the wrong reasons (false expectations of job security), their job security tends to increase!"[4] In other words, if leaders' ultimate goals are to save their particular offices in the congregation or their particular positions on a staff team, they may end up losing them! If, on the other hand, they forget about their own security in an effort to do whatever is necessary in order to strengthen the congregation, they will probably end up keeping their positions! "For those who want to save their life will lose it, and those who lose their life for my sake will save it" (Luke 9:24).

A faithful leader focuses upon the congregational family or the staff team rather than the individual jobs. Rigid job descriptions do not allow for the kind of personal growth that mentoring can produce and, as Bridges suggests, they do not allow for the flexibility needed in today's changing world. "If you have an organization full of job holders and a hierarchical framework to keep them in place, the traditional patriarchic leaders work fine. Or it does as long as the organization isn't exposed to a constantly and radically changing environment."[5]

If a leader desires to make mentoring the primary mode of leadership development within his or her congregation, it will be important for that leader to foster a culture of cultivation as opposed to a culture of competence. Strommen explains that within a competence culture, "One who wishes to be accorded esteem must demonstrate competence. Success is tied to being the best.... A church with a cultivation culture, *on the other hand,* wishes to see change, development, and growth in the people it serves. It is a culture dedicated to furthering the human spirit, to inculcating ethics and values, and to establishing a system of beliefs and expectations."[6] I agree that a culture of cultivation is much more malleable for mentoring relationships than a culture of competence.

### Characteristics of a Mentor

Leaders who strive to use mentoring as their primary means of staff development also espouse other characteristics. They possess healthy egos and have little need for individual strokes, or even clearly defined bases of power. I am not suggesting, however, that the development of such a team will nullify the need for a leader. Quite the contrary. A leader is essential to a well-functioning team. Gary McIntosh insists, "A team must have a leader. In nature two heads is freakish, and it is not good in the church. Whether in business, school, government or the church, there must be one head.... There must be a place of ultimate responsibility. There are so many situations in which someone must make the final decision."[7] While McIntosh and others assert that organizations must have leaders to make final decisions, ensuring that the buck stops somewhere is not the ultimate concern for the faithful leader. A colleague of mine, Jeff Jones, suggests, "The leader needn't be the one who retains ultimate authority. The leader can be a first among equals; the one who has the responsibility of enabling the team to function in a way that enables it to exercise authority. That is why the leader is needed, not just so that there will be someone to make the final decision."

Issues of power, credit, or praise cannot consume the leader who uses mentoring as the primary means of developing a congregation or a staff team. Effective mentoring teams mirror the formation of twenty-first-century business alliances. People operate out of whatever they bring to the table to contribute to the cause rather than the power or authority associated with their particular roles within the congregation. For a mentoring leader, this is true for everyone, including the leader.

Servant leadership also must be a part of the plan to develop a congregation or staff team through mentoring. Leaders who naturally exhibit servant leadership make excellent faithful leaders as well. The goal of mentoring is to help mentees develop to God's greatest potential for their lives. Mentors must discover what mentees need in order to grow and then provide those resources. Mentoring leaders truly believe that, given the right level of support, everyone has the potential to be strong contributors in the congregation. This level of support will require that a leader serve the ones whom she or he is leading. Although a certain level of technology is needed, often positive reinforcement and trust can do more to bring about effective, long-lasting personal growth and confidence than will tools and skills. "A lack of confidence will eat a mentee like an insect."[8]

Being able to see things that the mentee cannot see, the mentor provides the necessary support and encouragement to move the mentee along in unknown directions. "Now the Lord said to Abram, 'Go from your country and your kindred and your father's house to the land that I will show you'" (Genesis 12:1). Abram and Sarai journeyed to an unknown land. But, they also had a great deal of encouragement from God in order to do so. God constantly reminded Abram that he would become a father of many nations if he followed the unknown path. The mentor constantly says to the mentee, "I know that you do not think that you possess the skills to do this, but I have seen you work in similar situations, and I know that you can."

The goal of faithful leaders is to develop a strong congregation and a strong leadership team, rather than to be viewed as the strength or the brains behind the entire operation. Interestingly, several business leaders are promoting this faithful style of leadership as a successful style of future leadership. "I can imagine a day not long from now when succession at the top of firms may no longer be an exercise in picking one person to replace another. Succession could be the process of picking at least the core of a team."[9] Leaders who lead by mentoring will have the respect of their staff or volunteer team. Their team, in turn, will have the respect of their constituents.

### Making Mentors

Every leader should ask, "Is the process of developing the leadership potential of those around me an end in itself or a means to an end?" If the answer is "a means to an end" then the leader should not only strive to *mentor* those around him or her, but also should strive to *make mentors* out of those people.

Burroughs quotes an advertisement from *Southern Living* magazine: "She's only five, but she wants to help mommy with her garden. So you show her how to push the seeds into the soil with her tiny fingers and how to water them just enough so they'll flourish. Then, when the first sprouts appear, you can see her amazement at what she's accomplished. This year, instead of a garden, you've cultivated a gardener."[10] That is the goal of mentoring leaders. We are called not only to assist in the development of those around us. We are called to make others mentors. "Mentors are skilled in helping a mentee turn things around in their own lives first, and then, in the lives of others."[11] Jesus fully intended for the twelve disciples to disciple others. Jesus told the disciples they would do "greater works than these" (John 14:12). Inside every potential discipling or mentoring relationship lies a master teacher, discipler, or mentor.

Most mentoring relationships will end at some point in time. This circumstance, however, does not mean that all mentoring has ceased, only the previous mentoring relationship. Such occasions are sad but also serve as opportunities for the mentee to become a mentor for another. Except in the rarest of mentoring relationships, the mentee will foster an even greater amount of confidence and independence, once the mentoring relationship has ended. Many mentors and mentees who meet later in life meet as colleagues. Such collegial relationships are often sweeter and carry with them an indescribable appreciation of the previous mentoring relationship.

Faithful leaders are called to be mentors of others. They are also called to make mentors. Mentoring, like so many of God's treasures, has a way of perpetuating itself so that others may benefit from this particular gift of God.

1 Esther Burroughs, A Garden Path to Mentoring (Birmingham, Ala.: New Hope Publishing, 1997), 70.

2 Kennon Callahan, Effective Church Leadership: Building on the Twelve Keys (San Francisco: Harper & Row Publishers, 1990), 45.

3 Ammerman, Congregation and Community, 326.

4 David M. Noer, "A Recipe for Glue," in The Leader of the Future, ed. Frances Hesselbein, Marshall Goldsmith, and Richard Beckard (San Francisco: Jossey-Bass Publishers, 1996), 144.

5 Bridges, "De-Jobbed Organization," 17.

6 Strommen, 64–65.

7 Gary McIntosh, "Teaming in the 21st Century," The McIntosh 11, no. 6 (June, 1999), 2.

8 Burroughs, 70.

9 James F. Bolt, "Developing Three-Dimensional Leaders," 164.

10 Burroughs, xi.

11 Ibid., 29.

# 7

## CARING FOR THE SOUL

**A**LL LONG-TERM EFFECTIVE LEADERS LEARN TO take care of themselves. Faithful leaders learn to care for their souls above all else. No exceptions. The soul or *psyche* (as some prefer to use the biblical Greek term) is where God resides. Faithful leaders care for their souls in the same manner that one prepares for an honored guest. Faithful leaders welcome God as a guest rather than a visitor. A guest is both someone you are expecting and whom you would be pleased to have stay for a while. Faithful leaders hunger and thirst for God and know from experience that nothing else will satisfy.

## A Separate Category for God

Henri Nouwen, an icon for faithful leaders, challenged Christian leaders to go beyond relating to God as one among many relationships, but rather as our only relationship, in which all other ones are grounded.[1] For the faithful leader, spirituality is not merely one of the programs of the church. It is not merely a part of our weekly to-do list. It is not just something that we do if we have the time. It is not even merely the first thing that we do. It falls into its own category. Deepening our spirituality by caring for the soul forms the basis for all other activities. Over time, effective leaders learn to care for their entire beings. They take care of themselves physically, emotionally, mentally, and interpersonally. Faithful leaders add one more dimension and put it into a separate category. They do not put spirituality on a circle with all of the other aspects of life, allowing it to go round and round, hoping that it will stop long enough for them to catch a glimpse of it. No. God is not at the edge; God is the central focus for faithful leaders.

Our relationship with God falls into a separate category for good reason. No being other than God is timeless, spaceless, and dimensionless. God is able to be with us at all times, sensing our senses, inspiring our inspirations, and combating our discombobulations. Only God can turn back time and speed up tomorrow. Only God can reveal ultimate love, supreme power, and unfathomable wisdom; and even choose to reveal them simultaneously if desired. God deserves a separate category!

## The Source of Life

Because of God's unique attributes, God is able to be the source of our entire lives. Faithful leaders have discovered God's exclusive ability to be the spring of life and thus seek to derive all of their energy from God. For the faithful leader, the entire self-esteem package is wrapped up in one box labeled *spirituality*. The faithful leader knows that he or she is a child of God; and that's all that really matters. Faithful leaders strive to please no one other than God. No one else need be pleased with their actions. No one else need be displeased either. For faithful leaders, human relationships certainly become a means of satisfaction and joy, as well as occasions for sorrow and grief, but never a factor in the self-esteem formula. As Dietrich Bonhoeffer once stated, "Blessed is he who is alone in the strength of his fellowship and blessed is he who keeps the fellowship in the strength of the aloneness."[2] There is no dilemma in deciding whether to please God or humans. One relationship lies on the ring, the other at the center. Causing disappointments in relationships certainly can make life a mess; creating chaos at the center, however, can make the source of life a mess.

Faithful leaders have a strong internal locus of control. They do not believe that they are merely daily products of their surroundings. They believe in the power of God working through them to make any misfortune better, any celebration sweeter. They do not perceive their surroundings to be limiting. Nor do they perceive them necessarily to be life giving. Faithful leaders perceive their environment to be neutral, or at least of less influence than God.

Faithful leaders possess a great ego source: God. This ego source leads to great ego strength. They certainly understand that they have their personal needs, but make no attempt to meet those needs through their professional encounters. Pleasing others and receiving praise for it produces satisfaction for any leader. Serving God, however, provides the worth for the faithful leader. Thus, there is no need to succumb to the unrealistic expectations of others. Meeting God's expectations is the total focus. "The humble person ... seeks nothing for himself and has no fears for himself."[3] Being faithful leaders is not a matter of having tough skin; it is a matter of knowing the source of our esteem.

## Exercising the Soul

It is not easy to care for the soul. Often the small activities of life are more difficult than the major commitments that we make. I jokingly refer to this maxim as the "Peter Principle." Organizational theorists recognize the original Peter Principle as an intriguing theory that suggests that people within an organization typically rise to their level of incompetence. My Peter Principle also theorizes about incompetence, but draws upon the biblical narratives of the disciple Simon Peter. Remember when Peter told Jesus, "Even though all may fall away, yet

I will not" (Mark 14:29 NASB), and added, "Even if I have to die with You, I will not deny You!" (Mark 14:31 NASB). Peter, rather effortlessly, was able to make the life commitment. He readily professed his willingness to die for Jesus. Yet, later that same night, he denied even knowing Jesus! Sometimes the little commitments are tougher than the big ones. That's my version of the Peter Principle and it probably affects more of us than the old one. Many of us, as leaders, have made life commitments to God. Many of us also are intuitively aware of the colossal importance of doing the little things that will enable us to live out our life commitments. Yet for many faithful leaders, taking care of our souls, the most salient of all little things, is difficult to practice with consistency. Yes, the daily commitments can actually be tougher to keep than the eternal ones. That is my Peter Principle.

In order to care for the soul, we must exercise it as we would other parts of our body. Sweet suggests three activities for exercising the soul:

1. Daily alignment of ourselves with God
2. Daily reflection
3. Daily embodiment of the Spirit[4]

I present to you another three-fold formula for soul exercising. I admit that, although I have practiced the statement for years, I cannot recall the source of the following saying: Divert daily, withdraw weekly, abandon annually. I recommend this formula as a possible pattern to combat the new Peter Principle.

### Divert daily

Every day we must divert from the world's activities and spend some time with God, caring for our souls. Personally, I hold a mini-worship service each day. The form, and often the content, are derived from the Upper Room book, *A Guide to Prayer for Ministers and Other Servants.*[5] Each of my day's meditations includes an invocation, a Psalm, a Scripture reading, usually a Sunday lectionary reading, an excerpt from a devotional classic, reflection, prayer, usually a hymn, and a benediction. I certainly do not propose the mini-worship service as the

111

only possible format to use in caring for your soul. Each one must discover what works for her or him. But I believe that all faithful leaders will find a way to divert some daily time toward God. Without exception? Yes. You see, merely asking the exception question drifts us back into thinking that caring for our souls can be one of the many activities on our to-do lists rather than the source of all other activities. God is not something to be accomplished. God is the foundation of our lives! The Israelites were only allowed to gather enough manna for one day. The very next morning, they would arise and do it all over again. It took them forty years to learn to perform the task on a daily basis. For some of us, forty years is just about right! Sometimes it takes that long to exercise the practice of daily diversions with God.

I recant something I said earlier. I suppose there is one exception to the routine of daily devotions. Once a week, we are called upon to spend *an even longer time* with God! Not only should we divert daily. We also should withdraw weekly. For most Christians, the weekly worship service provides an excellent tool for the weekly withdrawal from the worldly routine. For other church leaders such as pastors, however, participating in the weekly worship service actually shortens the amount of time that they spend with God on that particular day. For those, the key component of the weekly time with God is that it differs in content rather than quantity. And that should be the goal for us all. Corporate worship can add a brand-new dimension to private worship. Caring for the soul in the company of others gleans insights from others' enlightenments.

Although corporate worship makes an excellent weekly withdrawal, most pastors will not be able to care for their souls if they are the primary one leading the weekly worship. If you perceive yourself to be in charge of the party, you will not be able to enjoy the festivities. Martha couldn't do it and neither can we. If you play the Martha role, you need to find some "Mary" time. One solution to finding an appropriate weekly withdrawal for pastors and other weekly worship leaders is simply to extend one of the daily worship meditations. The time for one or more of the daily components could be extended in order to meet the deeper needs of the soul. My goal during the weekly withdrawal is to "finish a conversation with God." Although God is completely unlike any other being, some of the ways that we maintain healthy human relationships work with God. My wife and I both have jobs that allow us to check in with each other on a regular basis. We also will occasionally meet for lunch, chat when we arrive home, etc. Even though we have daily conversation, we find ourselves saying, "We need to finish the conversation about that sometime." It is the same way with God. I find myself opening up new areas of my life each day in prayer. At least once a week, I try to finish one of the conversations that I began earlier in the week in prayer with God.

The third part of the formula challenges us to abandon annually with God. Some accomplish this third aspect through a personal retreat. The Upper Room resource mentioned earlier contains twelve monthly retreat models. Others I have known have abandoned annually by spending a day at a state park, going away for a "reading weekend," staying at a monastery, or attending a continuing-education event aimed at personal renewal. Just as we need at least one longer check-in time with God each week, eventually we need to set aside a few days with God in order to give God ample time to transform our souls.

We exercise the soul by giving God the time needed to care for it. No other activity will bring as much healing and renewal to our lives as spending quality time with God. That is because God is not another relationship. God is the source of life.

## Silence

Silence should always be part of the regular exercise regimen for the soul. "One of our main problems," Nouwen suggests, "is that in this chatty society, silence has become a very fearful thing."[6]

Silence can scare many people. Perhaps its ability to elicit fear is related to its ability to elicit the truth. It is not so much that silence works on us as it allows God to work on us. It is difficult for today's society to resist the temptation of filling a few seconds of silence with words, often meaningless words.

The Bible reveals God's pronouncements and instructions. Silence, however, produces the application and the transformation of those words. "Solitude is the furnace of transformation. Without solitude we remain victims of our society and continue to be entangled in the illusions of the false self."[7] Silence strips away the confusion, allowing the soul to become singularly focused.

The potential outcomes of silence: insight, acceptance, and transformation are all desired outcomes of the faithful leader. Silence can produce change, and the faithful leader has long since learned that change is not only necessary, but also desired. Silence can produce the sickle that divides the good wheat of the soul from the destructive tares of temptation. "Let him who cannot be alone beware of community. He will only do harm to himself and the community."[8]

There are times to speak and there are times to keep silent. Without times of devotion, reflection, and silence, leaders can burn themselves out. A balance must be kept between giving and receiving, speaking and listening. "When the door of the steam bath is continually left open, the heat inside rapidly escapes through it; likewise the soul, in its desire to say many things, dissipates its remembrance of God through the door of speech, even though everything it says may be good."[9] Leaders should build into their calendars both "crisis days" and "renewal days." Crisis days are blank days on the agenda to reflect upon the latest crisis. Renewal days are days set aside for caring for the soul.

What works for one in caring for the soul will not necessarily work for another. But faithful leaders find ways to renew their souls. If you have not embraced the discipline of silence, it can be a wonderful tool for soul renewal. Mozart once said, "I can tell a good musician by the way he plays the rests."

### Reflection

Like blood that runs through our veins, silence is the blood that runs through our souls. Both substances flow through and touch every life-giving corner. The two substances are similar in another way. Both have two forms of cholesterol. Both blood and silence can have good cholesterol and bad cholesterol. It seems odd that any substance would be desired in our arteries, but such a substance exists. Somehow good cholesterol makes the blood better. Likewise it seems odd to add anything to the beauty and simplicity of silence. But silence, like blood, has its own form of good cholesterol and its name is reflection. Silence, when combined with reflection, is a very useful tool. Transformation is a goal. Reflection creates a navigable intersection between silence and transformation. It uses silence in appropriate ways to transform our souls.

Effective leaders learn to reflect upon the past. Reflection helps us to make connections of past events in order to build our own magnified view of history. Richard Leider suggests, "Take a daily solo. An absolute essential for clear pictures is to allow at least fifteen minutes a day to reflect on the big picture and to set or revise priorities according to it."[10]

Reflection helps us make sense of the *stuff* in our lives. Reflection naturally leads to quality interpretation. Without reflection, we are left to interpret the events in our lives through the eyes of another. Reflection gives us control over our own interpretations. John Robert McFarland explains, "I'm the only one who has control of how I interpret events. I can see any occasion of my life as a 'bummer' or as an opportunity. It will be however I see it, because there is no outside standard by which to judge."[11]

"For now we see in a mirror dimly, but then we will see face to face. Now I know only in part; then I will know fully, even as I also have been fully known" (1 Corinthians 13:12). In this passage, the mirror is more problematic than the dimness. The problem with reflection is that it must be attempted from a human point of view rather than the vantage point of heaven. There is no way of changing that. We can, however, give God every opportunity to guide our reflections. That is why the best forum for reflection is in the midst of private worship, silence, and prayer.

The process of reflecting upon our lives with God is similar to the process of making a map of our life's past. C. S. Lewis claims that maps are essential for navigating either oceans or lives.[12] Reflecting upon our lives helps provide us with a sense of where to go next. Seeing where we have been provides great help in predicting where we should go next. If we can begin to see where past experiences have led us, we can better determine which experiences to pursue in the future.

Reflection is one of the staples for faithful leaders. Warren Bennis, one of the great authors of leadership material in the secular world, suggests that there are four lessons of self-knowledge. We can clearly see the importance placed upon personal reflection by Bennis in the four items below:

1. You are your own best teacher.
2. Accept responsibility. Blame no one.
3. You can learn anything you want to learn.
4. True understanding comes from reflecting on your experience.[13]

Reflection serves to develop healthy interpretations of our past experiences.

Reflection also makes more and more of our past appropriately available to those whom we serve as leaders. All effective leaders learn how to share personal experiences in order to encourage and comfort their followers. Sharing personal stories with a limited amount of reflection upon them, however, can lead to pure catharsis on our part and totally remove any leadership quality that may have been attached to the sharing of the story. "A preacher who wants to be a real leader is the *one* who is able to put the full range of life experiences in prayer, in conversation, and in lonely hours—at the disposal of those who ask *the person* to be the preacher."[14]

## Worry

Reflection provides the good cholesterol for the silence of the soul. Worry, on the other hand, is definitely bad cholesterol. Reflection differs significantly from worry; it produces new connections, elicits new insights, uncovers new pathways. Worry conjures the same images and dreaded consequences over and over again. We are challenged not to worry. Reflection appropriately uses the gold of silence. Worry tarnishes it.

Unfortunately, worry can occur quite naturally for leaders. As we discussed earlier, leaders make decisions on a regular basis. Leaders prioritize every day. One of the peers in my same position had some prophetic advice for me as I began my position, "You will be called upon to make more decisions," he said, "in less time and with less information than you ever thought possible." Leaders make decisions daily. Regrettably, this reality also surfaces the temptation to second-guess all of our decisions. Don't do it. It can turn an effective leader into a preoccupied leader and a faithful leader into a timid leader.

Don't sweat the small stuff. I know, that is easier said than done. "The world around us doesn't make it easy to give up sweating the small stuff," McFarland explains, "Many people put a lot of pressure on us to make sure we get the small stuff done. One of the reasons the world is in such bad shape is that we spend so much effort on the small stuff. It uses up all our energy."[15] Worry robs the soul of the beauty of silence.

All leaders are responsible for knowing something about a lot of things. Finances, management, team building, motivation, appraisal, human resources, policymaking, etc., are all part of the leader's portfolio. Christian leaders, however, might quite possibly be the worst dumped upon generalists. Most of the world believes that pastors can learn something from every other profession that exists. "Clergy often carry more baggage because they are greeted by a number of expectations for omnicompetence."[16]

Yet all leaders will make mistakes. Nothing ever occurs precisely as planned. Everything can be improved upon. "The human condition is one of weakness. This is why there are erasers on pencils. God has not equipped his animals and birds with infallible instincts. We human beings have to learn most things by trial and error... . The only real mistake is the one from which we have learned nothing."[17]

Allow me to spell out the dilemma that we have created thus far. Christian leaders are destined to be tempted to worry more than most leaders. It also is assumed that Christian leaders will be faithful leaders. Yet, throughout this book we have discovered that faithfulness requires more than exercising one of the many Christian options available to us. Faithful leaders don't just take the high road; they take the highest road. Thus, clergy are fraught with incongruous expectations. Even though they are prone to worrying more than most other professions, the world expects all of them to worry less as faithful leaders. It is precisely because of these incongruous expectations that clergy must not only agree with the concept of caring for the soul, they must practice the disciplines of caring for the soul.

# Awakening the Soul

It is relatively easy for God to get our attention. The Bible is full of examples. Burning bushes and people in blazing furnaces that will not be consumed, wood that will burn even when wet, seraphim with six wings, staffs that switch into serpents, rivers that get deeper as they trickle out into the tributaries, dead, dry, discombobulated bones that come back to life, good sweet wine from six stone water pots, and fast food from five loaves and two fish all work quite well as attention grabbers! What is difficult for God, however, is to maintain our attention long enough to focus upon life's deeper questions. Questions that include, "Why have you come here?" "What are you looking for?" "Where are you going?"

A closer scrutiny of the Scriptures reveals a pattern in the way that God interacts with humans. God regularly attempts to awaken our souls with a question. God challenges us by questioning us. If we grasp the deeper meaning of the question, good results usually ensue. If we, however, ignore the deeper meaning of the question, we usually are given more time and an appropriate place to ponder God's message. The more appropriate place usually comes to us in wilderness form. Wilderness times, however, are not something to be discouraged or dismayed about. Remember that God cared for the Israelites' every need in the wilderness, while he encouraged them to learn the daily discipline of focusing upon God.

Early on, Scripture reveals this questioning and response pattern between God and God's creation. In the third chapter of Genesis, God poses a rather obvious question to Adam. God asks a person in a rather unpopulated area, "Where are you?" I believe that God wanted Adam to focus upon where he was emotionally and spiritually as well as physically. Adam, however, avoids the deeper issues and blames his circumstances upon Eve. Eve, given the same opportunity, blames her circumstances upon God's created serpent.

Children learn from their parents. One chapter later in Genesis, we find God posing a question to Cain, "Where is your brother?" Cain, like his parents, becomes defensive. Both Cain and his parents are instructed to depart from God's presence, until they are ready to deal with the deeper questions.

In Genesis 16, God asks Hagar, who already has come into the wilderness, "Where have you come from and where are you going?" By dealing with the deeper meaning of the question, Hagar receives a blessing. In Genesis 37, we find Joseph looking for his brothers. Joseph has had yet another dream in which the sun and moon and exactly eleven stars bow down to him. He simply must inform his brothers. A messenger of God finds Joseph and asks, "What are you looking for?" Joseph, dealing only with the surface meaning of the question, ends up in a pit, in the wilderness.

In 1 Kings 19, God asks Elijah the same question twice, "What are you doing here, Elijah?" Whenever I was a child and my parents posed the exact same question to me twice in a short period of time, I knew that my first response must not have been sufficient for them. I always added more detail the second time. The first time, Elijah responds that he has been very zealous for God and that he alone is left from among God's prophets. When asked the question a second time, Elijah gives the same response. Immediately after Elijah's second response, God informs Elijah that he is being replaced by another prophet. Maybe it was something that Elijah said or maybe it was something that Elijah did not say, but God was not satisfied with his answer. Elijah did not deal with the deeper meaning of God's question.

What question is God posing to you as a leader? "What are you doing here?" "Where have you come from and where are you going?" "Do you love me?" "Who is your neighbor?" When God awakens our souls with a question, we will eventually be forced to deal with the deeper meaning of God's question. We can do it immediately, or we can be given wilderness time in which to ponder the question. The choice is ours. Ignoring God, however, is never an option.

Faithful leaders learn to care for their souls. Faithful leaders also learn to recognize moments when God is trying to get their souls' attention. Faithful leaders care for their souls above all else.

---

1 Henri Nouwen, A Cry for Mercy (Doubleday & Company, 1981).

2 Bonhoeffer, Dietrich, Life Together (San Francisco: Harper & Row Publishers, 1954), 89.

3 Ibid., 107.

4 Sweet, A Cup of Coffee, 49.

5 Job and Shawchuck, A Guide to Prayer for Ministers and Other Servants. 1983.

6 Henri J. Nouwen, The Way of the Heart, Desert Spirituality and Contemporary Ministry (New York: The Seabury Press, 1981), 59.

7 Ibid., 25.

 8  *Bonhoeffer, 77.*

 9  *Nouwen,* The Way of the Heart, *52–53.*

10  *Richard Leider,. "The Ultimate Leadership Task: Self-Leadership," in* The Leader of the Future, *ed. Frances Hesselbein, Marshall Goldsmith, and Richard Beckard (San Francisco: Jossey-Bass Publishers, 1996), 194.*

11  *John Robert McFarland,* Now That I Have Cancer I Am Whole, Meditations for Cancer Patients and Those Who Love Them *(Kansas City: Andrews & McMeel, 1993), 91.*

12  *Lewis, C. S.* The Joyful Christian.

13  *Warren Bennis,.* On Becoming a Leader *(Reading, Massachusetts: Addison-Wesley Publishing Company, 1989), 56.*

14  *Nouwen,* Creative Ministry, *38.*

15  *McFarland,* Now That I Have Cancer I Am Whole, *130.*

16  *Stewart C. Zabriski,* Total Ministry *(Bethesda, Md.: The Alban Institute, 1995), 66.*

17  *John Powell, S.J.,* Happiness Is an Inside Job *(Allen, Tex.: Tabor Publishing, 1989), 17.*

# 8

## NAVIGATING THE TEMPLATES

**A**S A SECRETARY WITNESSED MY STRUGGLE TO draft an office memo one day, she revealed to me yet another new computer trick.

"Why don't you use the template for that?" she inquired.

"What's a template?" I asked.

She proceeded to show me this nifty little tool for writing memos. The computer actually asks the operator to choose from among several types of memos, such as a professional memo, a contemporary memo, etc. Once a particular format is chosen, a form for the chosen document automatically appears on the screen. This form is called a template.

A template contains a set of fixed categories with numerous options within each category. What a wonderful tool! I no longer have to worry about whether or not I have remembered to include the date or highlight the subject. The template guarantees that I have included all of the necessary categories in order to write a complete memo. The template also, however, allows me great flexibility within each category.

In this chapter, we will look at several templates for Christian leadership. I use the organizational metaphor of a template as a set of fixed categories in which to apply creative leadership within each category. Why offer such categories? Because I believe that one of the aspects of faithful leadership is to strive for completeness within the congregations that we are leading.

122

## Called to Completeness

In Matthew 5:48, we read the words, "Be perfect, therefore, as your heavenly Father is perfect." Wow! Are we really called to be perfect? No. We are not. We are called, however, to be *complete*. Some suggest that a better translation of the Greek text in this passage might be, "Be complete, therefore, as your heavenly Father is complete." The Greek word *telos* that is used in this passage carries the meaning of fulfilling or being completed. It is the same word that Christ used on the cross when he said, "It is *finished*" (John 19:30, italics mine). It also is the same word used by Paul as he said, "Not that I have already obtained this or have already *reached the goal*; but I press on to make it my own … " (Philippians 3:14, italics mine). As Christians, we are called to be complete. I believe that also implicit in this command is an exhortation for Christian leaders to complete God's mission for whatever group or organization they are leading.

One way of striving for completeness is to "navigate the templates." Navigating God's templates involves two steps: (1) Naming the essential components of God's mission for the congregation or group that we are serving and (2) striving to find the most creative means available of accomplishing God's mission for each essential component. Establishing the templates for your congregation is a means of ensuring that you will not leave out anyone or neglect any task as you lead.

## Striving for Balance

Once the essential categories are established for your church, should you strive for balance among all categories? The answer is yes, but only over the long-term and only corporately rather than privately. I believe that a leader should strive for balance over time, drawing upon the entire range of membership available to the leader. It is not necessary to ask every member to be involved in every component, and it is not necessary for your church to produce activity in every component simultaneously. I'd recommend striving for corporate balance over individual balance and long-term balance over short-term balance. Over the long-distance journey, I believe that God calls faithful leaders to maintain a sense of balance among the various components or tasks given to the congregation. But, over the short term, it will be necessary for leaders to challenge the membership to become singularly focused upon a particular goal. In a similar manner, it would not seem helpful for a leader to ask every member within the group to maintain a balance among the essential components within the group. Each member will have distinct talents to be maximized during the various stages of his or her life.

One template that you will find below relates to the focus of ministry. When I pastored, I encouraged our church to maintain a balance within our focus of ministry, namely among our ministries to one another, our community ministries, our workplace ministries, and our global ministries. Over the short-term, however, one ministry was often highlighted over the others, and I never encouraged a member to be involved equally in all four categories of ministry. People would change over time. During the early years of adulthood, striving for ethical decisions in the workplace and ministering to colleagues was about all that some of our members could do. Later in life, their ministries often dealt more with the community. As they neared the senior years, ministry to one another in the church often became the primary focus. As a leader I emphasized balance, but over the long-term rather than the short-term.

In this book, I have talked a lot about prioritizing. Indeed, I believe prioritizing is the most common task that leaders face. I have tried to make it abundantly clear that a leader can only accomplish a limited number of tasks in a given period of time. In promoting prioritization, I have suggested that congregations have annual themes. I also have suggested that leaders break down the tasks that lie ahead for the week into an 80–20 ratio and seek to accomplish the high-impact 20 percent, knowing that there is a good chance that not all of the lesser-impact 80 percent items will get done. Focusing upon the majors rather than the minors is what effective leaders do. Faithful leaders, however, never totally neglect any portion of the mission that God has called the group to accomplish. Establishing the templates is a process of remembering that all of the work is God's mission and not ours. We should attend to our personal gifts and the gifts of our organization, but we cannot only do what feels good; we cannot only work on those tasks that will gather us praise. Establishing templates for our ministries is one of the ways that sets apart faithful leaders from merely successful leaders.

Establishing templates will not curtail creativity. Quite the contrary. As I discovered from my computer's template program, there are lots of options within each memo category. I can choose the font, the size, and the enhancement of the letters. I can alter the location, the column, and the angle of each message. I can add borders, details, and captions. What I cannot do is totally ignore the date, the salutation, and the other template categories. That is because every time I pull up the template program there is the date category and the salutation category staring back at me.

By establishing templates for a particular congregation, leaders tell members, "We will make numerous decisions about how we accomplish our tasks, but the set of tasks that we are called to accomplish are not optional." Offering options within, but not across the categories is the way to establish organizational templates. It is a way to stay faithful to all of God's people and all of God's mission.

## Sample Templates

As a starting point to establishing your organizational templates, I have provided several samples below. Each leader, however, should work together with the members to establish a workable template or set of templates for his or her group. As a committee leader, what do you believe to be the essential elements for your committee? As a pastor, what are the essential elements to being a congregation? As a new church planter, what must be in place in order to call yourselves a church? Do you need a building? Do you need a budget? Do you need a pastor? As you read through the sample templates, keep a pencil handy. Jot down other possible items to include in establishing the templates for your particular group. Rename or delete items in the examples that you find are not helpful. Space has been provided for your additions.

A role of leaders is to lead the development of a blueprint for the organization. The template may serve as the blueprint. No one builds a house by referring to the blueprints only once. A faithful leader will consistently refer to the set of blueprints and, at times, find it necessary to remind the group that they are neglecting a particular portion of the blueprint. Eventually all areas of the blueprint must be addressed in order to build the house.

### Template One: Spiritual Maturity

What are the categories that we absolutely cannot neglect if we are to grow into spiritually mature Christians? This particular template may serve as a starting point for a diaconate, a Sunday-school class, or any group responsible for encouraging the spiritual vitality of a group.
- Corporate worship
- Small-group involvement
- Daily devotions
- Ministry involvement
- 
- 

### Template Two: Resource Utilization

We are called to be stewards of many things. But what are the essential categories of stewardship or resource utilization? What has God given to us to take care of? This particular template might serve as a starting point for a stewardship committee or a mission board.

- God's image
- God's earth
- Our possessions
- Our talents
- The gospel
- Our thoughts
- Our actions
- Our world
- 
- 

### Template Three: Organizational Structure

What are the necessary components required to either birth or maintain your organization? A sample structural template for a congregation is described below. You may find this particular template to be quite bare. If you are tempted to add items, keep in mind the rules for adding a category to a template: the category must be absolutely necessary to the template. What is absolutely necessary in terms of your organizational structure? This particular template may be used by a local church council, a new church planting council, a ministerial association, etc.

- Energy source (for Christian churches this will be the Holy Spirit)
- Means of getting the energy source to the membership
- Means of adding new members
- Means of relating to other congregations
- 
- 

### Template Four: Organizational Health

There is a lot of emphasis today upon striving to be a healthy congregation. At its core framework, what does that mean? The following template keys upon the assumption that in order for an organization to be healthy, it must first be alive. Once alive, growth must occur. What aspects of health are absolute for your organization or, as the illustration below details, what components of your organization must be attended to in order for the entire unit to maintain health? This particular template may be used by any Christian organization.

- Minds (maturational growth)
- Bodies (organic growth)
- Hearts (incarnational growth)
- Actions (quantitative growth)
- 
- 

### Template Five: Organizational Function

What are the essential functions for your organization? What are the membership behaviors that define your organization? You may have established the structural components for your organization or congregation (as in template three), but what are the essential functional elements of your organization? Structures relate to form. Functions relate to behaviors. This particular congregational template may be used by a ministry board, a group of leaders within the organization, a board of directors, etc.

- Worship
- Evangelize
- Disciple
- Meet the needs of people
- 
- 

### Template Six: Organizational Focus

You may have established the structural and functional dimensions for your ministry, but what about the locus of your actions? Where should ministry take place? If you are not currently providing ministry to one

of the groups or in one of the locations listed below, are you neglecting someone? This particular template might be used by a ministry board, a mission board, an advisory council, etc.
- Ministries to one another
- Ministries in the community
- Ministries in the workplace
- Ministries around the globe
- 
- 

### Template Seven: Denominational Structure

What are the essential components necessary to birth or maintain a denomination? This particular template may be used by a denominational office, a judicatory office, an ecumenical office, etc.
- Means of connecting the congregations to one another
- Means of enabling congregations to work together on projects larger than themselves
- Means of caring for congregations and their leaders
- Means of supporting congregations in their ministries
- Means of enabling renewal of congregations and their leaders
- Means of adding new congregations
- Means of relating to other denominations
- 
- 

# Becoming a Faithful Leader

Becoming a faithful leader is not an easy process. The process calls for discernment, consistency, and integrity. The process can lead to great satisfaction as well as great struggle. Faithful leaders learn how to focus upon God's task for the moment all the while listening for

God's next set of instructions. Along the way, crises are viewed as opportunities and complacency is viewed as a challenge. Faithful leaders know that their role includes developing other faithful leaders as well as faithful followers. Even though there are moments when faithful leaders will feel totally alone among their peers and their followers; they also know that God is always present, encouraging, sustaining, and guiding. May God continue to bless your ministry and your leadership as you strive to become one of God's faithful leaders. Please know that I will be striving with you.

# BIBLIOGRAPHY

Allen, Loyd W. *Crossroads in Christian Growth*. Nashville: Broadman Press, 1989.

Allen, Roger E. and Stephen D. *Winnie-the-Pooh on Problem Solving*. New York: Dutton, 1995.

Ammerman, Nancy Tatom. *Congregation & Community*. New Brunswick, N. J.: Rutgers University Press, 1997.

Bandy, Thomas G. *Moving Off the Map: A Field Guide to Changing the Congregation*. Nashville: Abingdon Press, 1998.

Bardwick, Judith. "Peacetime Management and Wartime Leadership." In *The Leader of the Future*, edited by Frances Hesselbein, Marshall Goldsmith, and Richard Beckard, 131–140. San Francisco: Jossey-Bass Publishers, 1996.

Beckhard, Richard. "On Future Leaders." In *The Leader of the Future*, edited by Frances Hesselbein, Marshall Goldsmith, and Richard Beckard, 125–130. San Francisco: Jossey-Bass Publishers, 1996.

Bennis, Warren. *On Becoming a Leader*. Reading, Mass.: Addison-Wesley Publishing Company, 1989.

Bergner, Daniel. *God of the Rodeo: The Search for Hope, Faith, and a Six-Second Ride in Louisiana's Angola Prison*. New York: Crown Publishers, 1998.

Blanchard, Ken. "Turning the Organizational Pyramid Upside Down." In *The Leader of the Future*, edited by Frances Hesselbein, Marshall Goldsmith, and Richard Beckard, 81–88. San Francisco: Jossey-Bass Publishers, 1996.

Bly, Robert. *A Little Book on the Human Shadow*. San Francisco: Harper, 1988.

Bolt, James F. "Developing Three-Dimensional Leaders." In *The Leader of the*

*Future,* edited by Frances Hesselbein, Marshall Goldsmith, and Richard Beckard, 161–174. San Francisco: Jossey-Bass Publishers, 1996.

Bonhoeffer, Dietrich. *Life Together.* San Francisco: Harper & Row Publishers, 1954.

Bridges, William. "Leading the De-Jobbed Organization." In *The Leader of the Future,* edited by Frances Hesselbein, Marshall Goldsmith, and Richard Beckard, 11–18. San Francisco: Jossey-Bass Publishers, 1996.

Bryant, Charles. *Rediscovering our Spiritual Gifts: Building Up the Body of Christ through the Gifts of the Spirit.* Nashville: The Upper Room, 1991.

Bugbee, Bruce, Cousins, Don, & Hybels, Bill. *Network: Understanding God's Design for You in the Church.* Grand Rapids, Mich.: Zondervan Publishing House, 1994.

Burroughs, Esther. *A Garden Path to Mentoring.* Birmingham, Ala.: New Hope Publishing, 1997.

Callahan, Kennon. *Effective Church Leadership: Building on the Twelve Keys.* San Francisco: Harper & Row Publishers, 1990.

Covey, Stephen. *Principle-Centered Leadership.* New York: Simon & Schuster, 1992.

Covey, Stephen. "Three Roles of the Leader in the New Paradigm." In *The Leader of the Future,* edited by Frances Hesselbein, Marshall Goldsmith, and Richard Beckard, 149–160. San Francisco: Jossey-Bass Publishers, 1996.

Drucker, Peter F. "Not Enough Generals Were Killed." In *The Leader of the Future,* edited by Frances Hesselbein, Marshall Goldsmith, and Richard Beckard, xi-xv. San Francisco: Jossey-Bass Publishers, 1996.

Edelman, Marian Wright. *Guide My Feet.* Boston: Beacon Press, 1995.

Hawkins, Thomas R. Claiming God's Promises: A Guide to Discovering Your Spiritual Gifts. Nashville: Abingdon Press, 1992.

Heifetz, Ronald A. *Leadership without Easy Answers.* Cambridge, Mass. and London,: The Belknap Press of Harvard University, 1994.

Hudnut, William H. *Minister/Mayor.* Philadelphia: The Westminster Press, 1987.

Job, Reuben P. and Shawchuck, Norman. *A Guide to Prayer for Ministers and Other Servants.* Nashville: The Upper Room, 1983.

Jones, Laurie Beth. *The Path: Creating Your Mission Statement for Work and for Life.* New York: Hyperion, 1996.

Kelsey, Morton. *Encounter with God.* Minneapolis: Bethany House, 1972.

Kotter, John. *Leading Change.* Boston: Harvard Business School Press, 1996.

Kouzes, James M. & Posner, Barry Z. "Seven Lessons for Leading the Voyage to the Future." In *The Leader of the Future,* edited by Frances Hesselbein, Marshall Goldsmith, and Richard Beckard, 99–110. San Francisco: Jossey-Bass Publishers, 1996.

Leider, Richard. "The Ultimate Leadership Task: Self-Leadership." In *The Leader of the Future,* edited by Frances Hesselbein, Marshall Goldsmith, and Richard Beckard, 189–198. San Francisco: Jossey-Bass Publishers, 1996.

Marty, Martin. *A Cry of Absence: Reflections for the Winter of the Heart.* San Francisco: Harper & Row, 1983.

McFarland, John Robert. *Now That I Have Cancer I Am Whole: Meditations for Cancer Patients and Those Who Love Them.* Kansas City: Andrews & McMeel, 1993.

McIntosh, Gary. "Teaming in the 21st Century." In *The McIntosh 11, no.* 6 (June, 1999).

McKinney, William, Editor. *The Responsibility People.* Grand Rapids, Mich.: William P. Eerdmans Publishing Company, 1994.

Miller, Donald. *Reinventing American Protestantism: Christianity in the New Millenium.* Berkeley: University of California Press, 1997.

Miller, Herb. *The Vital Congregation.* Nashville: Abingdon Press, 1990.

Nash, Robert N. *An 8-Track Church in a CD World: The Modern Church in the Postmodern World.* Macon, Ga.: Smyth & Helwys, 1997.

Noer, David M. "A Recipe for Glue." In *The Leader of the Future,* edited by Frances Hesselbein, Marshall Goldsmith, and Richard Beckard, 141–148. San Francisco: Jossey-Bass Publishers, 1996.

Nouwen, Henri J. *Creative Ministry.* Garden City, N.Y.: Image Books, 1971.

Nouwen, Henri J. *A Cry for Mercy.* New York: Doubleday and Company, 1981.

Nouwen, Henri J. *The Way of the Heart: Desert Spirituality and Contemporary Ministry.* New York: The Seabury Press, 1981.

Peck, M. Scott. The Road Less Traveled. New York: Simon & Schuster, 1978.

Powell, John, S.J. *Happiness Is an Inside Job.* Allen, Tex.: Tabor Publishing, 1989.

Rendle, Gilbert. *Leading Change in the Congregation.* Bethesda, Md.: Alban Institute, 1998.

133

Sample, Tex. *The Spectacle of Worship in a Wired World: Electronic Culture and the Gathered People of God.* Nashville: Abingdon Press, 1998.

Sample, Tex. *White Soul: Country Music, the Church, and Working Americans.* Nashville: Abingdon Press, 1996.

Schaller, Lyle E. *The New Reformation: Tomorrow Arrived Yesterday.* Nashville: Abingdon Press, 1995.

Senge, Peter M. *The Fifth Discipline: The Art and Practice of the Learning Organization.* New York: Doubleday, 1990.

Smith, Douglas K. "The Following Part of Leading." In *The Leader of the Future,* edited by Frances Hesselbein, Marshall Goldsmith, and Richard Beckard, 199–208. San Francisco: Jossey-Bass Publishers, 1996.

Strommen, Merton P. *The Innovative Church: Seven Steps to Positive Change in Your Congregation.* Minneapolis: Augsburg, 1997.

Sweet, Leonard. *A Cup of Coffee at the SoulCafe.* Nashville: Broadman & Holman Publishers, 1998.

Ulrich, Dave. "Credibility x Capability." In *The Leader of the Future,* edited by Frances Hesselbein, Marshall Goldsmith, and Richard Beckard, 209–220. San Francisco: Jossey-Bass Publishers, 1996.

Warren, Rick. *The Purpose Driven Church: Growth Without Compromising Your Message & Mission.* Grand Rapids, Mich.: Zondervan Publishing Company, 1995.

Watkins, Wyatt T. *Gospel, Grits, and Grace: Encountering the Holy in the Ridiculous, Sublime, and Unexpected.* Philadelphia: Judson Press, 1999.

Wheatley, Margaret J. *Leadership and the New Science: Learning about Organization from an Orderly Universe.* San Francisco: Berrett-Koehler Publishers, 1992.

Woods, C. Jeff . *We've Never Done It Like This Before.* Bethesda, Md.: Alban Institute, 1994.

Zabriski, Stewart C. *Total Ministry.* Bethesda, Md.: The Alban Institute, 1995.